Traditional Buildings of Britain

An Introduction to Vernacular Architecture and its Revival

R. W. Brunskill

CASSELL
in association with
PETER CRAWLEY

To Mimi, Lesley, John, Lorna, Cameron,
Rory and Robin (but not forgetting Charlie)

First published in Great Britain in 1981
in association with Peter Crawley
by Victor Gollancz Ltd
Seventh impression 1989
New edition published 1992
First paperback edition published 1993
Third impression 1999
New retitled edition published 2004
in association with Peter Crawley
by Cassell
an imprint of the Orion Publishing Group Ltd
Wellington House, 125 Strand, London WC2R 0BB

A catalogue record for this book
is available from the British Library

ISBN 0-304-36676-5 (hardback)
      0-304-36667-6 (paperback)

Printed and bound in Great Britain by
Butler and Tanner Ltd, Frome and London

www.orionbooks.co.uk

Contents

Illustrations

Chapter 10

Chapter 11

Key

GM—Grant Muter
HA—Hallam Ashley
NM—Nigel Morgan
HBC—Halton Borough Council
NMR—National Monuments Record, English Heritage (formerly Royal Commission on Historical Monuments of England)
PJME—Peter Eyres
PSC—Peter Crawley
RCAHMW—Royal Commission on the Ancient and Historical Monuments of Wales
RWB—R. W. Brunskill
WHW—W. H. Woodruffe

Craythorne House, Tenterden, Kent
This very attractive building is quoted by John Newman (in *Buildings of England—
West Kent and the Weald*) as one of the two best examples of eighteenth century
Tenterden vernacular. Built just before 1790 it is an imposing four-square house,
actually timber-framed but faced with boarding cut and painted white to simulate
masonry. As a building which combines local traditions with some
acknowledgement of contemporary fashionable architecture it is a fine example of
the vernacular architecture which abounds everywhere—not only in Kent.

Preface and Acknowledgements

Over 30 years ago I wrote a book (*Illustrated Handbook of Vernacular Architecture*, Faber & Faber Ltd., 1970) intended as a field guide for those who probably had some familiarity with architecture, but who were interested in extending their knowledge of vernacular buildings in Britain. During the following decade more and more books, booklets, journals and articles about vernacular architecture appeared. Some were concerned with specific building types, some with building materials, some with regions or districts, single villages or parishes or even individual buildings. Several, including two backed by the resources of the then Royal Commissions on Historical Monuments, were devoted to the vernacular architecture of whole countries. At the same time, in no small part due to the influence of television, there had been a surge of public interest in architecture, and it was with this in mind that my publisher, Peter Crawley, suggested that there was a need for an introductory work on the subject. This would take the potential enthusiast for vernacular buildings along those first steps which would lead him to the level of books such as the *Illustrated Handbook of Vernacular Architecture* and, it was hoped, some way beyond. *Traditional Buildings of Britain* was the result and I hoped it would meet that need.

In the decade after its publication interest in architecture, including vernacular architecture, increased still further and it seemed timely to revise and expand the book to make it even more useful as an introductory work. More sketches and photographs were added, some photographs were changed, the bibliography was expanded and brought up to date and a new chapter was added on vernacular interiors.

Now a further edition seems necessary. Some changes in photographs have been made. The bibliography has been extended and re-cast. The main addition however, has been a new chapter about the Vernacular Revival and its influence on houses of the present day.

It is only right that my first acknowledgement should be to Peter Crawley, for, not content with proposing the book, he made himself responsible for providing the greater part of the photographs. Acknowledgement is also due to the National Monuments Record of England for three photographs retained in this edition. Illustration no. 8 is from the National Monuments Record for Wales through the courtesy of Peter Smith when Secretary to the Royal Commission on the Ancient and Historical Monuments of Wales. Illustration no. 50 is from a photograph by Hallam Ashley FRPS and no. 109 from a photograph by W. H. Woodruffe. I am also grateful to former students Peter Eyres and Grant Muter for photographs nos. 95 and 113 respectively and to the former Halton District Council for no. 49, and to Nigel Morgan for photographs nos. 16 and 75. I have taken the remaining photographs and have prepared all the sketches. To reviewers of earlier editions I must acknowledge the benefit of their comments. To all my friends and fellow students in the Vernacular Architecture Group I must make general acknowledgement for all I have learned from them and apologise for whatever they may think is over-simplified in this book. Finally, I must thank my wife and daughters for their forbearance as each edition was prepared.

R. W. Brunskill
Wilmslow, 2004

Introduction

This is a book about buildings. It is not about the great and imposing buildings which we usually call works of architecture, but about the smaller and less pretentious buildings which are far more numerous and which provide an essential background for the great architectural works. It is about houses: not about palaces and mansions nor about semis and slums but about cottages and farmhouses, dwellings of the ordinary people of town and countryside, designed and built when the individual family could feel it had some direct influence on the nature of its own home. It is about barns and windmills and factories: not about tin sheds or steelworks but about the buildings which used to house simple farming activities and about industries in which muscle power or the harnessed power of natural elements, such as wind and water, largely governed the nature of the industrial processes and the shape of the buildings which enclosed them. In short it is about the buildings which we have come to call vernacular architecture.

The book sets out to discuss in very general terms where examples of vernacular architecture can be found, when they were placed there and why. It attempts to point out, again in very general terms, what house plans or barn plans or windmill plans were adopted by people of different social levels at different times and why. It points out what building materials were available and considered appropriate for the generations of Jacks who built houses for themselves and stables for their horses. It comments briefly on the types of simple ornament, bold perhaps but never gaudy, with which our ancestors gave character to their cottages and barns. It hints at the classification which is as necessary to the study of buildings as to birds. One hopes that it will suggest the excitement of spotting a two-unit baffle-entry house as something to be compared with that of the first sighting of a great spotted woodpecker! The text also gives a few general hints on dating the buildings. Dating is a process which provides a constant challenge and in which even the most expert may be confounded.

This is also a book about regional personality as expressed in buildings. By word and sketch and photograph it distinguishes between the long low houses of granite and thatch which grow from the weather-beaten turf of Dartmoor and the pert houses of timber and plaster and tile which cluster in villages in Norfolk and Suffolk. It gives indications of the elements making up regional, even local character which is still strong in a small country displaying more variety in a drive of ten miles than one of a thousand kilometres elsewhere.

In any book about buildings various technical terms have to be used. Some of them, such as 'chimney breast' and 'chimney pot' are familiar enough to everybody. Others, such as 'double-hung sash window' simply describe a feature which is itself familiar even if its technical description may be unfamiliar. The drawings in the Introduction show some of the terms which have been used. The remainder are described and illustrated in succeeding chapters.

The illustrations—sketches and photographs which form a major part of the book—are planned to amplify the text, but may also stand on their own. The sketches are also intended to help with observation: once an item has been seen on a building it may be checked and then it will be remembered. The photographs—most of them taken specially for the book—provide a continuous commentary on the totality of vernacular architecture, reminding the reader that while it may be convenient to separate plan, section, constructional material and architectural decoration we are not looking really at baffle-entry, or coursed rubble, or king mullions but at complete buildings intended for the habitation of real people, real cows and really clattering looms.

There will be little here about preservation. It is hoped that understanding will lead to appreciation and in turn to a wish for preservation, or rather conservation, of our stock of vernacular buildings. Preservation simply of what remains of tumbledown cottages or obsolete granaries is rarely feasible and only desirable to a limited extent. Conservation in the sense of repair, adaptation and improvement of buildings to give them a new lease of life is what is needed more often. Thoughtless conservation of the type which induces a loving owner to replace the sash windows of a rural farmhouse by bow windows modelled on the shop windows of an urban market place is to be deplored. With greater understanding of the vernacular architecture of a region a more sensitive response may prevent such gaffes in the future.

Although the scope of the book is wide it must be stressed that it is only an introduction. It aims to stimulate the latent and emerging interest in vernacular architecture, to encourage readers to make their own observations, to discover what research is being done and to provide a basis for further reading in the more specialised books which are now being published.

Illustrated Glossary

The term 'vernacular architecture' has been used by architects, historians, archaeologists and critics since as long ago as 1839 to describe the minor buildings of town and countryside. It remains the most appropriate term and is increasingly often adopted not only by those professionally or academically concerned with old buildings but also by those members of the general public, ranging from school children to active pensioners, who appreciate buildings but are suspicious of jargon. However any study involves classifications, statements of general principle, description and discussion of examples and the use of some technical terms is unavoidable. Some are traditional, some are used in the study of buildings of all grades, some have had to be invented to help in the study and appreciation of vernacular buildings. A selection of those most often used appears in the following diagrams and then a number have been applied to a photograph of a work of vernacular architecture.

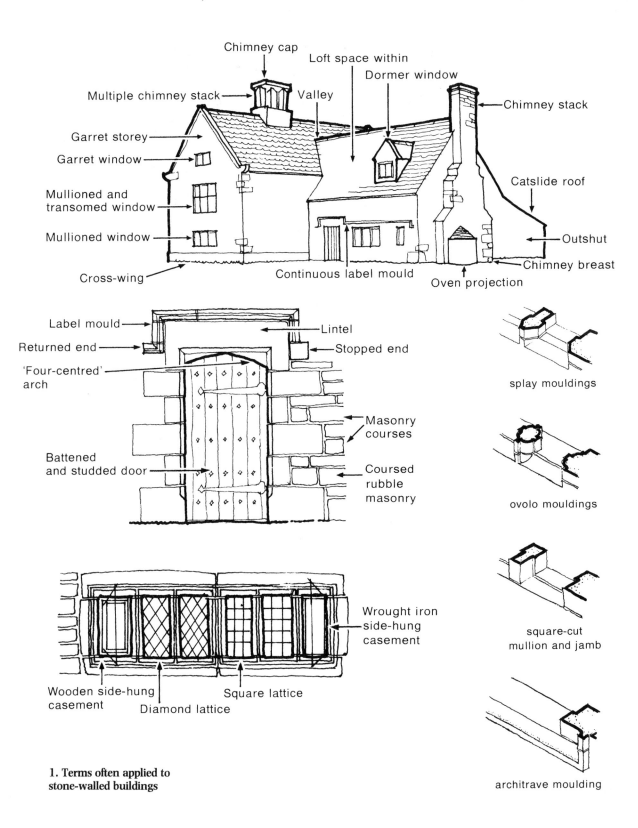

Chimney cap

Loft space within

Dormer window

Multiple chimney stack →

Valley

Chimney stack

Garret storey →

Garret window →

Mullioned and transomed window →

Mullioned window →

Catslide roof

Outshut

Chimney breast

Cross-wing

Continuous label mould

Oven projection

Label mould →

Lintel

Returned end →

Stopped end

'Four-centred' arch

Masonry courses

Battened and studded door →

Coursed rubble masonry

splay mouldings

ovolo mouldings

square-cut mullion and jamb

Wrought iron side-hung casement

Wooden side-hung casement

Square lattice

Diamond lattice

architrave moulding

1. Terms often applied to stone-walled buildings

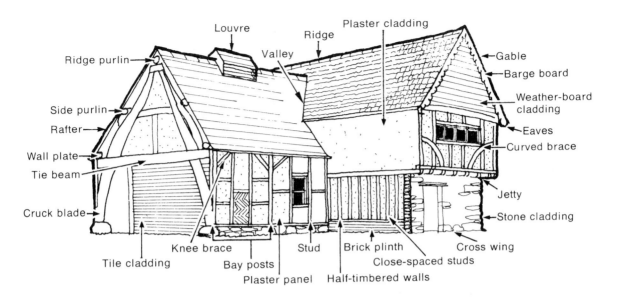

Louvre

Ridge purlin

Side purlin

Rafter

Wall plate

Tie beam

Cruck blade

Tile cladding

Knee brace

Bay posts

Plaster panel

Stud

Half-timbered walls

Valley

Ridge

Plaster cladding

Gable

Barge board

Weather-board cladding

Eaves

Curved brace

Jetty

Stone cladding

Cross wing

Close-spaced studs

Brick plinth

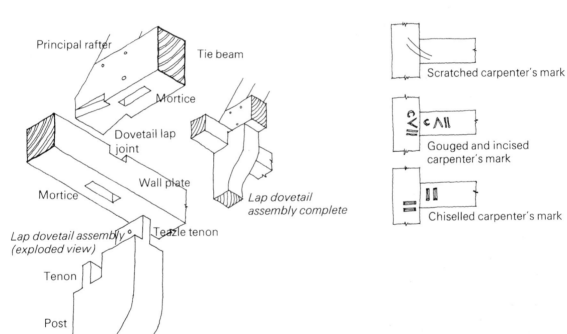

Principal rafter

Tie beam

Mortice

Dovetail lap joint

Mortice

Wall plate

Lap dovetail assembly complete

Lap dovetail assembly (exploded view)

Teazle tenon

Tenon

Post

Jowl

Lap dovetail assembly where post, tie beam and wall plate meet

Scratched carpenter's mark

Gouged and incised carpenter's mark

Chiselled carpenter's mark

2. Terms often applied to timber-framed buildings

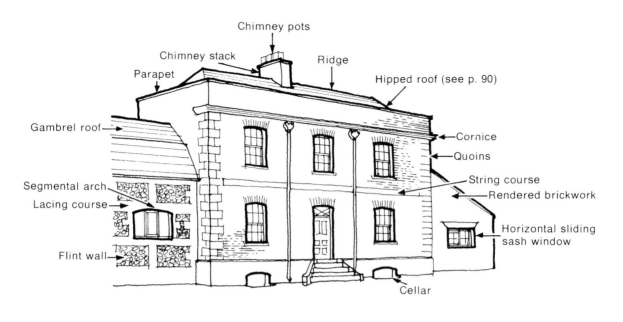

Chimney pots

Chimney stack Ridge

Parapet Hipped roof (see p. 90)

Gambrel roof

Cornice

Quoins

Segmental arch

String course

Lacing course

Rendered brickwork

Flint wall

Horizontal sliding sash window

Cellar

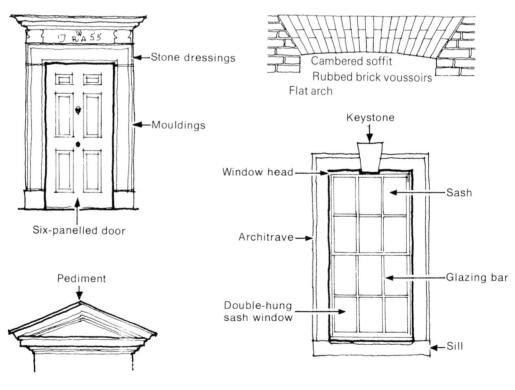

Stone dressings

Mouldings

Six-panelled door

Cambered soffit

Rubbed brick voussoirs

Flat arch

Keystone

Window head

Sash

Architrave

Glazing bar

Double-hung sash window

Pediment

Sill

3. Terms often applied to brick-walled buildings

Bed

Half brick (Half bat)

Stretcher face header face

Closer

18

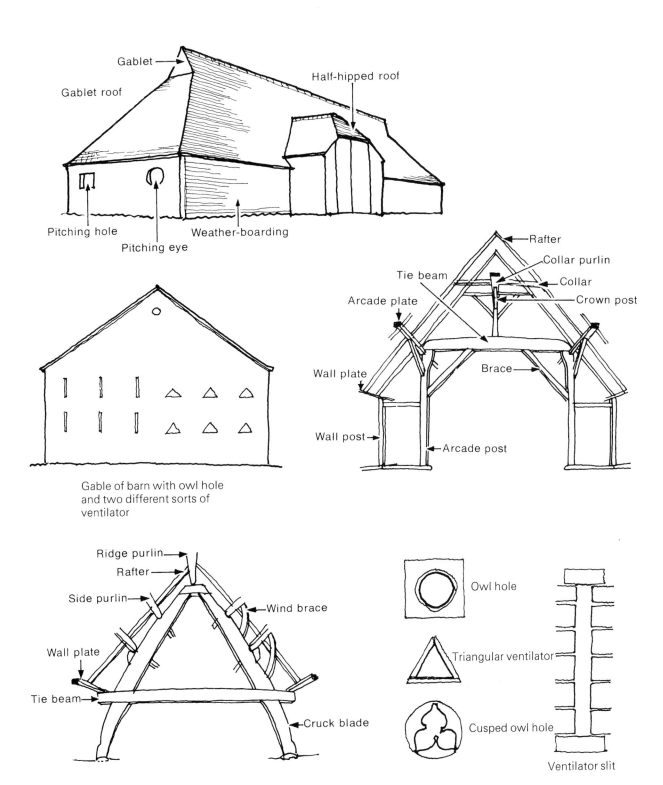

Gablet

Gablet roof

Half-hipped roof

Pitching hole

Pitching eye

Weather-boarding

Gable of barn with owl hole
and two different sorts of
ventilator

Rafter

Collar purlin

Collar

Crown post

Tie beam

Arcade plate

Brace

Wall plate

Wall post

Arcade post

Ridge purlin

Rafter

Side purlin

Wind brace

Wall plate

Tie beam

Cruck blade

Owl hole

Triangular ventilator

Cusped owl hole

Ventilator slit

**4. Terms often applied to
farm buildings**

Chapter 1
What is vernacular architecture?

Since this book is about cottages and farmhouses, barns and cow-houses, water mills and oast-houses it suggests that there must be something in common, something shared by all these building types. In this chapter we will look at these common features and see why the term 'vernacular architecture' has been adopted to define them.

There are indeed certain characteristics which these buildings have in common and which they do not share with other buildings. In common is the satisfaction of simple demands of family life, farming ways, and industrial processes in buildings which are traditional in design, though subject to gradual innovation, are built out of materials near to hand, and appear to belong to the district or region in which they are found and to no other. They are quite distinct from those buildings whose design is dominated by a concept such as power or mystery, which are designed by professionals according to rules agreed by theorists in academies, and which are built of materials selected the better to match the concepts enshrined rather than simply to take advantage of what might be lying around waiting to be used.

Let us take two extreme examples to illustrate the point. At the beginning of the eighteenth century a traveller to the Highlands of Scotland might have seen a small group of crofters' cottages rising to meet the demands of a precarious life based partly on fishing and partly on primitive agriculture. The small cluster of buildings would have consisted of stones and soil shifted from the fields and piled into low walls, then covered with a roof of turf or rough thatch. The work would have been done by the crofter families with the barest minimum of skilled assistance and following long-established traditions. At the same time a traveller to London would have seen St Paul's Cathedral rising from the ashes of the Great Fire to meet the demands of the reformed catholic religion in the nation's capital. The building would enshrine preaching and ceremony in a setting full of symbolism according to designs prepared by Sir Christopher Wren, a former Professor of Astronomy, which gave his personal version of a Renaissance style used throughout Western Europe and already taken across to America. The cathedral was being erected from Portland stone laboriously quarried and transported from Dorset and covered with lead expensively smelted in Derbyshire. The two buildings shared a date and little else.

But let us take two less extreme cases. In the early seventeenth century Cotswold farmers were apparently sufficiently prosperous through a combination of productive agriculture and the developing textile trades, to invest in property. They built for themselves houses of soft, honey-coloured stone and delicate stone tiles, with mullioned windows and moulded doorways, and assembled them in farmsteads and villages which we all find unusually appealing. They constitute the major part of what we are happy to call the architecture of the Cotswolds. At the same time there was designed and erected the Queen's House (which now forms part of Greenwich Hospital) as a dainty country retreat for Queen Henrietta Maria. The architect, Inigo Jones, used all the skills which he had learned from study and measured survey on his European journeys and produced what is unquestionably a work of architecture—though one of quite small size. The Queen's House may be of higher quality than the anonymous Cotswold farmhouse, but can we deny that they are of the same order, that Pevsner's 'conscious aesthetic intention' can be detected in the one as well as in the other?

If one is prepared to accept that both groups of buildings attempt architecture rather than mere building, then what distinguishes the crofter's cottage and the Cotswold farmhouse from the Queen's House and St Paul's Cathedral must surely be that the former buildings are following the traditions of the people as found in particular places, while the latter buildings are following the academic rules understood by a cultured few whose home is wherever an international cultural movement is accepted. One set of buildings may be described as 'folk' or 'vernacular', the other as 'academic' or 'polite'.

At this point the analogy with speech has been introduced. The older among us, at least, can distinguish between vernacular and polite speech. Speaking in the vernacular, a person deals with concrete matters with the aid of a limited and backward-looking vocabulary of words picked up from here and there and put together without much thought for grammatical rules, and in a manner which, as dialect, is taken to belong exclusively to a limited district or region. Using polite speech his socially superior neighbour deals in abstractions with the aid of an extensive and forward-looking vocabulary of words, some newly culled from Latin or Greek roots, organised with strict grammatical correctness and in a manner which is shared with all others of the same select group wherever they may be found. Vernacular speech is the equivalent of the crofter's cottage and the Cotswold farmhouse as well as the Cumbrian bank barn and the Lincolnshire pumping windmill; polite speech is the equivalent of the cathedral, the palace, the monastery and the town hall.

However the distinction is less a matter of polarity than of degree. If we take a single building type, such as the domestic, we can see that there are grades between the obviously vernacular and the obviously polite: between the labourer's cottage and the monarch's palace there are the farmhouse and the gentleman's residence, the house of the superior yeoman and the house of the small manorial proprietor. Whether one is vernacular or polite is a matter of degree rather than of absolutes. It is a matter varying with social status but it is also a matter varying with time. If one takes the case of a substantial farmer housing his family, and maybe one or two servants, then any house he built in, say, 1650 is likely to be generally accepted as vernacular, whereas if he built in 1750 the label would be less firmly applied as fashionable influences were detected; building in 1850 he would probably have a farmhouse in the fashionable Gothic Revival style designed by a professional man (perhaps with the aid of pattern books) and built out of bricks and slate and softwood timber brought along the newly-opened railway line. To some extent, and at the moment it is not possible to be precise, the distinction between vernacular and

6. House and cottage at Collyweston, Northants. This pair of buildings provides an excellent example of vernacular architecture. The buildings house ordinary domestic activities, they are simple and unpretentious in design but lack neither good proportions nor appropriate ornament. They are certainly not the most outstanding buildings in Collyweston but join with other vernacular buildings in providing an agreeable background to life in that community.

polite is also a matter of place. The farmer in Western Wales or the Western Isles of Scotland stuck to the old traditions long after the farmer of Kent or Sussex had thrown over his own traditions and come to expect a farmhouse which we would accept as a work of polite architecture.

There is one further element which should be added to the vernacular/polite distinction and, again, it is in some ways a matter of degree. This lies in the extent to which a building was intended to be permanent. On the face of it this seems an odd concept to introduce into any consideration of architecture in Britain: an expression 'as safe as houses' does not seem to accord with any idea that a house might be so flimsy and deliberately ephemeral that it could be blown down with 'a huff and a puff'. It is not, of course, an odd concept to introduce into any study of the architecture of minor buildings in Africa, and many other parts of the world, where it seems to be considered natural that buildings should not be intended to last. The term 'primitive' has been used for such buildings—not in any sense as a term of condemnation of the buildings or the societies which produced them, but simply as a convenient word of description. Buildings which are comparable were once widely erected in this country; as they are no longer standing we are not concerned with them architecturally, though they may have great archaeological interest. There is, however a distinction which may be made between 'primitive buildings' and 'vernacular architecture' and if we add this to the distinction between 'vernacular' and 'polite' then we can see vernacular architecture as occupying a zone part way between the extremes of the primitive and the polite.

The changeover from building for a limited life to building for an indefinite life is one of the aspects of what we have come to call 'The Great Rebuilding', a phenomenon which occurred between the late sixteenth century and the early eighteenth century in most of England and Wales and part of Scotland for people at the social level of the ordinary farmer. For the person of manorial or minor gentry status the changeover seems to have occurred two or three hundred years earlier. For the poorer families the cottages were built in permanent materials from the mid-eighteenth century onwards in much of the countryside, earlier in many towns and economically more advanced counties, later in extremities of Britain and in most of Ireland. A Great Rebuilding occurred in the farmyard too, and one in which class and status also had its effect: the horse and the ox were housed in permanent quarters long before the pigs or the poultry could expect to be so favoured.

The Great Rebuilding was not necessarily one of complete new construction. It seems that sometimes a new house might have been built on old foundations, sometimes an obsolete plan was modernised in new construction, sometimes a timber-framed building of conventional plan was clad in newly available or newly fashionable materials and sometimes the existing building was retained as a wing or appendage to a newly built house. Nevertheless, in whatever form the evidence is to be found it is clear that buildings of permanent construction demonstrate from end to end of the country that something we can recognise as a housing revolution or a Great Rebuilding did occur.

It is interesting to note that British settlement of the North American colonies occurred at a critical time in the development of Small House and Cottage design. There was, therefore, a sort of Great Rebuilding overseas. However, the influence of different cultures introduced by various immigrants to the colonies and the effect of different environmental conditions meant that American design soon diverged from British origins.

And so the term 'vernacular architecture' has been adopted to define that sort of building which is deliberately permanent rather than temporary, which is traditional rather than academic in its inspiration, which provides for the simple activities of ordinary people, their farms and their simple industrial enterprises, which is strongly related to place, especially through the use of local building materials, but which represents design and building with thought and feeling rather than in a base or strictly utilitarian manner.

Chapter 2

What sorts of vernacular buildings are there?

Examples of vernacular architecture may be found among domestic buildings, farm buildings, minor industrial buildings and certain other building types. The most popular, and to most people the most interesting, are undoubtedly the houses; farm buildings are proving to be increasingly popular and are increasingly under threat; minor industrial buildings have for many years been studied as examples of industrial archaeology through their connection with industrial processes; certain other building types have been accepted, though not universally, as coming under the heading of vernacular architecture.

Broadly speaking, all houses built for people of other than very high status and erected before the second half of the nineteenth century are generally considered to come within the vernacular province. We have seen that Great Houses of the rich and powerful are to be excluded, as works of polite architecture. So are the Small Houses and Cottages of the late nineteenth and twentieth centuries. Their traditional characteristics of planning and use of material had been overwhelmed through the influences of fashionable design, disseminated in cheap journals and pattern books, and the use of other than local materials, through the effects of a national transport system which, at last, allowed the swift and cheap movement of building materials from point of origin to point of use. The Large Houses of people of local importance, such as the resident medieval Lord of the Manor, or the favoured clergyman of the eighteenth century, or the large scale farmer of the early nineteenth century, usually have the characteristics we call vernacular. The Small Houses of yeoman or customary tenant farmers of the sixteenth and seventeenth centuries, of farmers on other tenancies of the eighteenth and nineteenth centuries, and indeed of anyone with some reasonably secure rights in land are also usually called examples of vernacular architecture. The Cottages of craftsmen and labourers, of people who gained a precarious living from two or three seasonal occupations, of people who depended on charity of family or neighbours are also considered as vernacular buildings. Some almshouses are so closely related to local building traditions as to fall under this heading, but many sets of almshouses were erected by wealthy patrons using professional designers, and are just as much examples of polite architecture as other dependencies of the Great Houses.

Houses in towns, as well as those in the countryside, may be examples of vernacular architecture. It is fair to say that the urban equivalent of the property of a member of rural society will be vernacular or polite in architecture as it would in the countryside. Thus the town house of a gentle family occupying a Great House in the village will be a work of polite architecture, whereas the house of a middling merchant or a substantial shopkeeper or a weaver or smith

a. Large House

b. Small House

c. Cottage

d. Barn

e. Stable

f. Granary/cart shed

g. Cow-house

h. Dovecot

i. Field barn

j. Hay barn

k. Windmill

l. Watermill

m. Kiln

n. Chapel

o. School

7. What sort of vernacular architecture? Drawings indicate representative examples of domestic, agricultural, industrial and other types of building.

8. Tredegar House, Dyffryn, Monmouthshire This Great House shows the very opposite of vernacular architecture: it is architect-designed, it was up-to-date in its planning and architectural detailing, it was one of the first buildings to be erected in brick in South Wales and it has no features that tie it to Monmouthshire rather than any other part of Britain.

will be the urban vernacular counterpart of the Small Houses and Cottages of the countryside. In England and Wales, dwellings in the form of flats are too recent in construction to be called vernacular, but this is not true in Scotland, where the tradition of living in 'tenements' in the towns is very old-established. Generally, traditions were rather different in towns, opportunity for regional variations was rather less, and pressure of innovation is always assumed to be greater on town houses than on those of the countryside.

We sometimes forget that for every farmhouse on the farmstead there are usually several farm buildings and so there may well be more vernacular farm buildings in total than there are vernacular domestic buildings. Those farm buildings, which were designed on traditional lines and have local characteristics, fall under the same definitions as vernacular houses. Thus the ordinary barn, stable, cow-house, granary, shelter shed, pigsty etc. is the equivalent of a Large House, Small House and Cottage according to its size and according to the status of the activity which it housed. It seems that the accommodation and processing of grain crops had a higher status than the mere storage of hay and so a threshing barn was usually a more carefully designed building than a hayloft or Dutch Barn; similarly, a horse had considerably more status than a hen, so all stables were much better designed and constructed than poultry sheds (though not necessarily any better than dovecots, many of which are popularly believed

9. Cottage near Ampney St. Peter, Gloucestershire
This is an example of domestic vernacular architecture: it provides a simple, direct, architectural response to the very basic requirements of the domestic life of a cottager. It follows tradition in planning but borrows its simple architectural decoration from more up-to-date buildings; it employs the stone of the locality for both walls and roof.

to have been designed by Inigo Jones). The grade of farm building would also tend to follow the grade of farmhouse, so that the massive barn, which often rivals the manor house which it serves, may be considered as Large among farm buildings whereas the tiny barn of a part-time farmer/part-time lead miner is the Cottage equivalent. The large scientifically-planned farmsteads of the mid-nineteenth century are works of polite architecture, as are the stable blocks which form part of the architectural composition of great country houses. The great feeding sheds and silos of modern farm buildings are, of course, not vernacular and few would consider them architecture though they can be quite dramatic incidents in the landscape. For different reasons the temporary shelters run up out of bales of straw are not works of vernacular architecture: they are the agricultural equivalent of primitive buildings.

Vernacular industrial buildings comprise those mills and kilns, factories and warehouses in which simple industrial (or sometimes commercial) demands have met with a traditional response in building. Under this heading one may include those in which the building shape was largely dictated by the source of power—windmills are the obvious example, or the way in which power was transmitted—water-powered corn mills or textile mills, for instance, or one may include those, such as pottery kilns or glass-making kilns, in which the process

10. Granary at Williton, Somerset
This is an example of agricultural vernacular: there was a need to store grain in conditions protected from the weather, well-ventilated but dry, protected from attack by vermin. The result is a compact single-storey structure, of timber-frame under a stone-tiled roof, raised for ventilation on staddle stones whose shape deters rats.

11. Buildings at Lynch, near Allerford, Somerset
This brewhouse and malting kiln remind us of the very small scale of industrial and commercial enterprises at one time and the way their buildings followed local traditions.

12. Methodist Chapel, Heptonstall, Yorkshire, W.R.
Built in 1764 by the local congregation according to the ideas of John Wesley and enlarged later so as to give two longer sides to the octagonal plan, the chapel has the gritstone walls and slated roof common in the village.

largely determined the shape; one may include those storage buildings in which the material to be stored—coppice timber for bobbin making, charcoal for smelting for instance—determine the general shape of the building. Although new industrial requirements were coming forward throughout the early days of the Industrial Revolution they were initially met with the aid of whatever was closest in traditional precedent and with the use of traditional building materials; to this extent the buildings may be considered as within the realm of vernacular architecture. Once the buildings were scientifically designed by engineers, or seen as an opportunity for formal composition and decorative display by architects, their vernacular characteristics were diminished or lost.

Among the other buildings which some people consider to be examples of vernacular architecture are the very simplest village churches, such as one may find still in remote valleys of upland England, and the even more simple early non-conformist chapels. The early Quaker and Unitarian chapels of certain parts of the North of England, and the late but humble Methodist chapels of

13. Guildhall, Lavenham, Suffolk
This is a vernacular public building erected for the Guild of Corpus Christi, probably shortly after 1529. The design, construction and decoration are similar to those of the domestic buildings of this market town.

much of Wales, as well as the small meeting houses of East Anglian Dissenters, all owe more to the traditional design and construction of houses and barns than they do to the relatively sophisticated design of parish churches firmly in the mainstream of the development of polite architecture in Britain.

It must surely be agreed that there are many building types represented under the heading of vernacular architecture. Although, quite reasonably, we tend to concentrate on domestic buildings, it is important to remind ourselves that these other types provided the architectural setting for the domestic, they were in every sense complementary, and that it is no accident that the term 'house' is used in connection with religious (meeting house), industrial (engine house) and agricultural activities (cow house) as well as with the purely domestic.

Chapter 3

Where are the different vernacular buildings likely to be found?

Vernacular buildings in the countryside

Since vernacular buildings are so numerous they should not be difficult to find, and, on the face of it, any excursion into town or countryside should bring an embarrassingly large number of examples for study. Indeed this is so, and sheer numbers present as much of a problem as an opportunity. Yet vernacular buildings are also found in odd places, and it is as well to examine locations and sites in a little more detail.

Almost certainly, more people will find the vernacular buildings of the countryside command the most immediate attention. They are congregated in villages, clustered in hamlets, grouped in farmsteads or completely isolated; their location provides evidence for the total study of the landscape and in turn may be explained by all sorts of settlement factors. In many parts of the country the earliest settlements likely to be of interest are the communal settlements of village and hamlet—even the isolated farms of Wales and Scotland are often the solitary remnants of such groups. Perhaps we should look first at the standard English village beloved of film makers and detective story writers.

Such a village contains a parish church and a baron's castle or squire's mansion, both examples of polite architecture. Then there may be found the manor house, long used as a farmhouse, the parson's rectory, one or two of the largest farmhouses; they are all vernacular Large Houses. The farmhouses and most of the farm buildings are clearly vernacular, as are the oldest cottages which fill the spaces between the farmsteads. The water-powered cornmill on the outskirts of the village is a vernacular building but the redundant railway station and goods warehouse are not. Neither are the council houses round the curve of the road as it enters the village, nor the National School and its prefabricated extensions, but the little Methodist chapel, on a tiny piece of ground not quite in the village, may well be a piece of vernacular design.

Villages such as these are generally strung out along a wide street or arranged to enclose a village green: in some cases they are actually decayed market towns and the street or green was the market place; in most cases the street or green provided a common grazing or exercise area and, as old photographs show, the present tarmac and kerbstone roadway has little relevance to the original use of the space. If the village has remained well-populated then there may be a continuously built-up frontage to street or green; if it has decayed then visually the boundaries will be very loosely defined; if it was decayed and has become a prosperous commuter village then the gaps between the vernacular houses will have been filled with newer houses and as these may be of Vernacular Revival inspiration one must be careful to distinguish between the genuine and the derived features.

14. Lower Slaughter, Gloucestershire
Vernacular buildings of one broad period may be seen in this part of the village. Generally each house seems to occupy the front of its own toft, but some buildings are at right angles to the green through which the stream flows.

Each farmstead or house in the village would be located on a toft, that is a piece of land occupied exclusively by the farmer or householder and distinct from the communally-tilled fields or the village green and surrounding waste land subject to communal rights. On this toft were the farmhouse and farm buildings, garden and orchard, midden and cess pit. The toft usually stretched from the communal street or green back to the boundary of the fields, the backs of the crofts being sometimes linked by a lane or footpath. Normally the toft was narrower than it was long, but if population had pressed on the village then it might have been subdivided once or twice, in which case it would be very narrow indeed and tightly packed with buildings; alternatively a decayed village might show signs of amalgamated tofts with buildings very loosely spaced. Until quite recently it was customary to face houses towards the sun rather than necessarily towards the street. Where the village ran roughly east–west then the houses would fill the width of the toft, one range facing the green or street, the other side backing onto this communal area. Where there was a north–south arrangement for the village then houses tended to run along the plots, at right angles to the street. If tofts were wide then there was some choice of arrangement available to the builder: if tofts were narrow then only

15. Wisbridge Villas, Tavistock, Devon
This group of cottages was built as a hamlet serving workers at the local mine.

one position might be available for the house. Quite plainly there were many factors which affected the use of the tofts and historians are by no means certain that all the factors are known, let alone understood. Excavation of villages is suggesting that there was more movement of house sites on the tofts than was at one time assumed.

As the bonds of tradition loosened, prospect became more important than aspect and houses and cottages with names like 'Belle Vue', 'Beaulieu', 'Prospect Cottage' etc. were sited to give the best view from the dwelling—and usually the best impression of the house at the same time.

Some buildings appear to occupy odd positions in the village. At the entrance one finds the cottages of the 'town-headers', poor people suffered to squat on square pieces of land of dubious ownership and little value; communal buildings such as school or pound were built on the green and here, also, cottagers were sometimes allowed to establish squatters' rights.

The line between village and hamlet is very difficult to draw. Generally a village has a church, but many churches occupy ancient sites distant from clusters which everyone would accept as villages, while the very large northern parishes had many townships, some of which were of village size and only one of which housed the parish church. Some hamlets, and especially those which are really decayed villages, have tofts arranged as described for villages; other hamlets, and especially those which have grown up from early colonisation of the waste, consist of apparently haphazard collections of buildings, sometimes inexplicably closely intermingled, and with no detectable pattern. To complicate understanding further there was the practice of farming separately from a communal farmyard in what has been called the 'unit system'.

Isolated farmstead settlements are of four main types: those resulting from reclamation (or assarting) of the waste land, those surviving from larger groups now decayed, those making permanent a temporary occupation and those deliberately planted as part of improved subdivision of the land. The process of carving a farm from the wilderness applied just as much to medieval England as to nineteenth century America. The heavily forested damp clay land of Essex or the wild inhospitable fells of Westmorland can show evidence of ancient farmsteads, moated or part fortified, surrounded by irregular rounded fields transformed by generation after generation of farming into a landscape which now appears warm and inviting in the case of Essex, and neat and acceptable in the case of Westmorland. Wales is full of isolated settlements, some formed in this manner, others the token of the ebb and flow of settlement as a family group established itself, grew into a village, worked out the land, or otherwise decayed, and then declined, to leave only the single farmstead. Scotland, Wales and upland England can provide instances of summer pastures being turned into year-round farms, the sites of the hafoty and the shieling, which accommodated the herdsmen, being occupied by permanent farmsteads. Probably the most numerous group of isolated farmsteads comprises those established in the eighteenth and nineteenth centuries, after transhumance had been abandoned, at a time when there was intense pressure of population on the land and for cultivation to supply the enlarged towns. To some extent isolated farmsteads were established on enclosed common fields but mostly the waste land between

16. Scotch Green Farm, Goosnargh, Lancashire
This former farmhouse stands isolated in the Lancashire countryside.

villages which had provided poor quality permanent pasture was divided and enclosed. Compact new farms were set up, each one comprising squarish fields and with the farmstead in the centre. Some of the later examples are altogether too formally designed to be called vernacular but most are quite legitimately counted under this heading.

Looking out over the countryside one can see the villages and hamlets set at regular distances from each other, each having its quota of poorer land and water meadow. On higher ground above this line of settlement there are zones in which isolated farmsteads are found, waves of population pressure encouraging the extension of cultivation onto land which was less naturally fertile but was free from the customs and restrictions of the land around the villages. On still higher ground there may be the signs of mineral working, engine houses or furnaces remaining as tokens of the ephemeral exploitation and settlement. From the same viewpoint one can see the signs of settlement retreating as population pressure diminished or agricultural demand was met from other sources, as seams were worked out or as more economically worked deposits were found. Walls and fences tumble in, bracken overwhelms grass, forest plantations creep down the slopes, farmsteads fall into ruin. Within the villages one farmstead takes the place of half a dozen, one shed serves the purpose of half a dozen specialist buildings, one tractor and its attachments replace half a dozen labourers with forks and shovels, and half a dozen cottages become redundant. These are the circumstances in which vernacular architecture demands to be studied.

Having briefly noted some of the factors affecting the locations of vernacular buildings, a little closer attention may be paid to siting. One aspect of some interest is the relationship between the various buildings of the farmstead, reflecting as it does, once again, the delicate balance between function and fashion. In the first place the farmhouse could be integral with the farm buildings, very little difference being seen between the walls and roof which protected the family and those which housed the stock. It could be attached to one of the farm buildings but in such a way that domestic and agricultural uses were clearly differentiated, or it could be detached but overlooking the farmyard or completely detached, paying no more regard to the rest of the farmstead group than a great country house pays to the home farm on which it depends. In the second place the buildings themselves may be loosely arranged in apparently accidental disposition, or carefully placed around a foldyard or midden; they may avoid steep slopes or seek them out so as to allow gravity to reduce labour; they may nestle in folds in the ground or they may stand out proud as if defying the elements.

We like to think that climate has had a great influence on the siting and design of vernacular buildings. In certain obvious instances this must be so: a windmill must be on a hilltop to catch the wind just as a watermill must be in the valley bottom where the water flows. In other instances climatic influences on siting may be reasonable but difficult to prove: did the villages of the Yorkshire Dales cluster houses tightly together to keep out the cold winds, to provide protection from raiders or because of the demands of an increasing population on a limited amount of building land? Can the long, low, ground-hugging lines of a crofter's cottage or a Devonshire longhouse really represent a response to seashore gales when houses in inland sites look just the same? Do farmhouses avoid the skyline because such sites are windy or because a lower, more sheltered position is also more central to the fields?

Vernacular buildings in towns

Within the towns there are broadly three zones of settlement of interest in the study of vernacular architecture: the ancient core, early ribbon development and housing areas newly established in the eighteenth and early nineteenth centuries. As in the countryside there are many buildings which are works of polite rather than vernacular architecture—cathedrals and the churches of once rich city parishes, town halls and hospitals, banks and department stores, railway stations and art galleries. But there are many more which are vernacular rather than polite: town houses, artisans' workshops, labourers'

17. Near St. Columb Major, Cornwall
This engine house stands isolated at the head of a former mine shaft in the Cornish tin mining district. The simple rectangular shapes and rough local stone betray its location.

37

18. North Brink, Wisbech, Cambridgeshire
Houses, mainly three storeys in height, make a continuous frontage overlooking the river and give an essentially urban appearance.

cottages, certainly, but also timber-framed ranges hidden behind modern façades. The buildings reflect in siting, planning and construction early pattern behind the superficially up-to-date appearance which they present on street façades.

In the ancient core of a typical city or market town the burgage plots or building sites were long and narrow, stretching from the street and market place back towards the river, the walls, or some other part of the town. Every foot of frontage was commercially valuable, every foot of depth provided building land to be used as population increase or commercial expansion demanded. Usually it was necessary to provide access within each plot to its own backland. There were various arrangements of hall and kitchen, workshop and sales area, but the tendency was for the front of the plot to be built up higher and higher and the depth to be built up deeper and deeper, either with a succession of transverse buildings separated by courts or light wells, or with a line of buildings fronting onto a passage or alleyway. During the past two hundred years or so there have been layers of fashionable elevation applied to the frontage but buildings hidden in the depths have been little altered. Within the past few years more drastic redevelopment of sites has meant the loss of some buildings but the revelation of others previously hidden.

Only a small part of each ancient town was so heavily built up; old town maps show that other parts were full of wide plots with orchards and gardens behind. This was especially true of the early ribbon development along the roads leading to the gates through walls mostly long demolished: towns like Beverley and Stamford as well as Chester and York are still approached by way of houses of the Georgian urban vernacular filling their wide frontages on tree-lined roads.

Industrial and commercial development of the later eighteenth and the nineteenth centuries put pressure on the towns even more than on the countryside. In some cases the cottages for the workers were squeezed into the burgage plots along alleys and passageways leading from the streets. In others cottages were built in terraces on larger plots between the lines of ribbon development as land became available. Often the terraces were built to a continuous frontage around hollow squares containing privies and drying yards. Sometimes the rather larger cottages made circles and crescents around churches or parks. By the later nineteenth century such houses and industrial buildings were works of polite rather than vernacular architecture, but many towns, especially in the North and Midlands, can show fifty or a hundred years of vernacular cottage design.

Of course the distinction between town and country has been diminishing for some time now. The distinction was blurred during the Industrial Revolution when pitheads and colliery settlements imposed a sort of town layout and scale in remote places, and water-powered textile mills brought strips of terraced housing to the valleys of the Pennines and the Cotswolds. More recently the spread of suburbs around the larger towns, encouraged by trains and trams, buses and cars has brought a sort of countryside into the cities. But this spread has meant that ancient villages and hamlets have been captured within the city boundaries and it is still possible to find eighteenth century settlements down unlikely lanes and seventeenth century farmsteads engulfed in twentieth century suburbs.

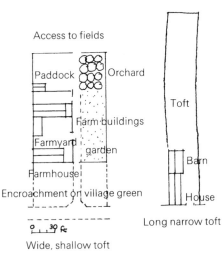

18a. Village site plans

18b. Urban site plans

Village site plans

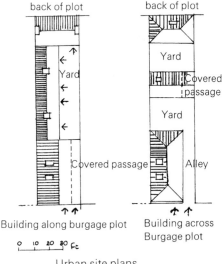

Urban site plans

Chapter 4

Some typical examples of vernacular buildings: plans and sections

In this chapter we shall look at certain types of building in more detail, considering first the general tendencies, changes and improvements in their design which took place over the centuries, and then examining some selected examples. We shall look at them in plan and cross-section. Most people are familiar with building plans: anyone who has measured a room for a carpet or looked around a housing estate with a set of builders' plans will be familiar with the small scale representation of what a building would be like if it were sliced horizontally and seen from above. The cross-section is less familiar, though, again, anyone who has measured a room for a set of curtains or a built-in wardrobe will be familiar with the representation of what a building would be like if it were sliced vertically and seen from alongside. The plan and cross-section together show the volume of the building and the spaces housing various activities. From the plan and section are derived the elevations, the views of the building seen from outside, looking at the front or back or looking at either of the ends. The simple plan and section emerge from a straightforward study of the building such as an architect or archaeologist might prepare (indeed, plan and section are major tools in the investigation of the history of any building which had several phases of construction). Such a study does not in itself reveal what activities the various spaces were intended to house; we decide these by reference to historical sources either directly applicable to the building in question or giving information by analogy with comparable buildings. Archaeological and historical studies together suggest that while functions were obviously major factors in the design of these simple vernacular buildings, tradition and fashion were also very significant, though in changing proportions. Tradition was more important in the earlier buildings as they developed from the primitive to the vernacular, and fashion more important in the later buildings as they developed from the vernacular to the polite in architecture.

Houses and cottages

If we look at the plans and sections of houses we can see that the basic requirements were a place for living (including cooking, eating and meeting people) and a place for retiring (including sleeping and storage of valuables). The living place was more public, the retiring place was more private; more space was required for public than for private use; as now, so in the past, more waking hours were spent in public rather than private activities. These two spaces required at least one source of heat, and walls and roof had to keep in the heat

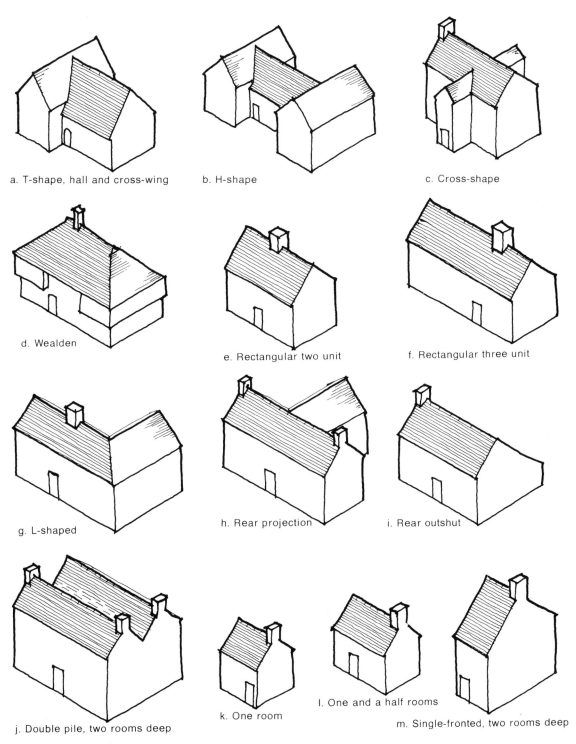

a. T-shape, hall and cross-wing

b. H-shape

c. Cross-shape

d. Wealden

e. Rectangular two unit

f. Rectangular three unit

g. L-shaped

h. Rear projection

i. Rear outshut

j. Double pile, two rooms deep

k. One room

l. One and a half rooms

m. Single-fronted, two rooms deep

19. What shape is the house?

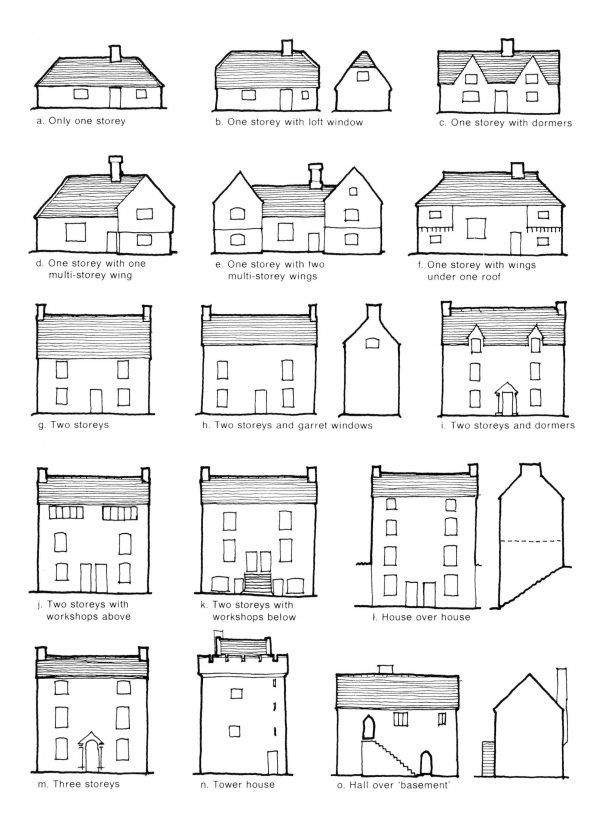

a. Only one storey

b. One storey with loft window

c. One storey with dormers

d. One storey with one multi-storey wing

e. One storey with two multi-storey wings

f. One storey with wings under one roof

g. Two storeys

h. Two storeys and garret windows

i. Two storeys and dormers

j. Two storeys with workshops above

k. Two storeys with workshops below

l. House over house

m. Three storeys

n. Tower house

o. Hall over 'basement'

42

and keep out the weather. It is important to remember that one thinks of the activities and the consequent plans and sections first and the means of sheltering those activities second. A door was needed for access, windows for light (and, at one time, both were necessary for control of the draught to the fire). Walls, roofs, and chimneys together with doors and windows were essential for every house, but gave the opportunity for development and individual expression in the infinite variations on standard plans which provide much of the fascination in vernacular houses.

The basic two-unit, single-storey house-plan was the starting point for developments which eventually led to the diminution and then the extinction of vernacular characteristics in domestic architecture. From this starting point there was a tendency for usable floor area to increase: if one compares the floor area occupied by a farmer in the seventeenth century in his crude single-storey house with that occupied by his descendant in a two-storey farmhouse with garrets and cellars then some idea of the increase may be obtained. More rooms came to be provided as a consequence of increasing specialisations: the single retiring room spawned multiple bedrooms, parlour, dining room, study, not to mention pantries and granaries. There was a trend towards increased comfort, for more rooms to be made usable through improved heating. The single hearth recorded in houses subject to the Hearth-Tax in the late seventeenth century became at least four fireplaces, each one a more efficient heating device, in the house of a century later. There was an increase in privacy in the home: family and servants were able to keep to separate zones even in quite small houses, rooms no longer opened off each other but off corridors or staircase landings. There was a tendency for functions formerly performed out of doors or in rough shelters to be brought within the envelope of the house: thus kitchens, sculleries, dairies, came into the house—perhaps in various wings and subsidiary sections, but still recognisable within the house. The effect of all these changes was, as we have noticed, to increase the floor area and the number of storeys. At the same time the tradition of the long, low, ground-hugging dwelling house, which applied at most levels of society, was overwhelmed by the fashion for tall imposing façades marking several storeys of tall rooms in deep cubiform buildings. There was also the rather curious development of a differentiation in status of the different parts of a house as seen from outside: front and back were not much different in the medieval house but the organisation and detailing of the front of an early nineteenth century house was much superior and more up to date than that of the rear.

The study of vernacular architecture in this country has progressed far enough now for some classification of house plans to be devised. Not all vernacular houses conform to the simple classes but many more do than do not. A small selection from the classes is described and illustrated here.

Is it an H-shaped Hall House?

By the middle of the fifteenth century the plan of the medieval manor house had reached a certain degree of standardisation, consisting as it did essentially of a single-storey hall with cross-wings at each end to give an H-shaped plan.

Many such houses still had an open hearth, though by now the standard plan included a fireplace in the rear wall serving equally the 'upper' and 'lower' ends

20. How many storeys has the house?

43

21. H-shaped Hall house: Little Moreton Hall, Cheshire

This is an unusual view of the well-known Little Moreton Hall which shows its origin as an H-shaped Hall house. The hall is in the centre, the service wing on the right and the private wing on the left. A brick chimney stack serves a hall which was originally open to the roof, later floored and now an open hall again.

of a hall in which such a social distinction had been established. At the upper end the high table was placed on a slightly raised dais or platform and was protected from draughts and enhanced in importance by a deep canopy above. At the lower end the screens passage ran between front and back doors and gave access between fixed screens or partitions to the hall. Doors leading from the dais gave access to private dining rooms or parlours with chambers above. Doors leading from the screens passage gave access to buttery, kitchen passage and pantry on the ground floor and a staircase leading to the principal chamber or bedroom on the first floor. The first floor rooms of the two wings were normally quite separate, each served by its own staircase. Tall windows, sometimes fully glazed, sometimes with glazing above and shutters below rose from the side walls to give plenty of daylight into the hall; the ground floor rooms in the cross-wings had quite small windows or ventilation slits but the upper floor rooms were well illuminated by traceried windows.

The general arrangement of hall and cross-wings is easily recognised from the outside. The heating arrangement in the hall gave rise either to a louvre in the roof (if there were an open hearth), a massive chimney breast but a fairly slender chimney stack (if there were a fireplace at the rear), or a much less imposing chimney arrangement coming through the ridge in the cases in which the

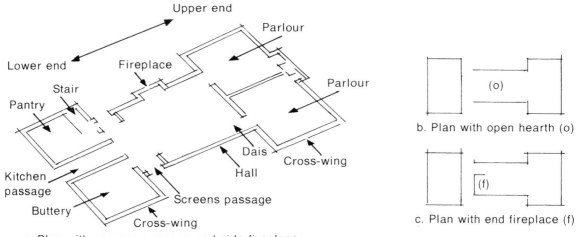

Upper end

Lower end

Parlour

Parlour

Fireplace

Stair

Pantry

Dais

Kitchen passage

Cross-wing

Hall

Buttery

Screens passage

Cross-wing

a. Plan with screens passage and side fireplace

b. Plan with open hearth (o)

c. Plan with end fireplace (f)

d. Open hall and cross-wings

e. Floor inserted in hall

f. Cross wings battlemented

g. Hall, cross-wings and porch

22. Is it an H-shaped Hall house?

fireplace serving the hall had been arranged to back onto the cross-passage. Subsidiary rooms either had no fixed heating or had side-wall fireplaces.

Few such H-shaped halls survive unaltered, of course. The most common improvement was the insertion of an intermediate floor and extra fireplaces to give a comfortable low-ceilinged hall on the ground floor and a new heated great chamber above. The long low window on the ground floor and the long or square window above marked by a confident, sometimes well-decorated dormer are outward signs of this transformation.

One variation common in the Border Counties was to take up one or even both cross-wings as a defensible tower with thick walls and battlements. A late version of the H-shaped hall plan, found especially in the Yorkshire Pennines, retained the open hall, lit by a large mullioned and transomed window extending practically the length of the front wall, and approached from a highly decorative porch.

Is it a Wealden House?

Among the earliest substantial dwelling houses for people of the yeoman farmer class which survive are those which are usually called Wealden Houses because they were first recognised on the Weald of Kent and Sussex. Houses of this type

23. Bayleaf, Singleton, Sussex
This Wealden house, called Bayleaf, has been re-erected as part of the Weald and Downland Open Air Museum. The house was probably first built in the fifteenth century and the fireplace and chimney stack which were added in 1635 have been removed so as to show the original arrangement.

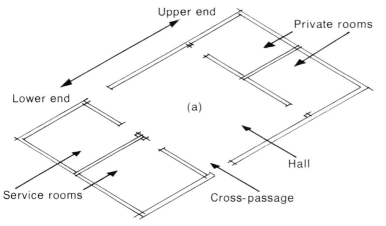

Upper end

Private rooms

Lower end

(a)

Hall

Service rooms

Cross-passage

a. Plan with cross-passage and open hearth

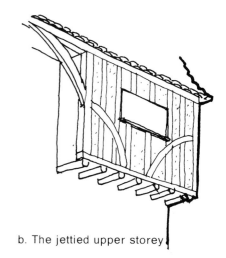

b. The jettied upper storey

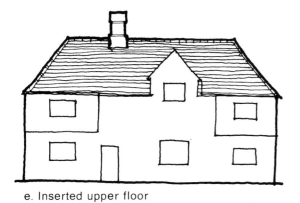

c. Elevation of a typical Wealden

d. Half-Wealden of the towns

e. Inserted upper floor

f. New brick façade

24. Is it a Wealden house?

can, in fact be found in all the counties of the south-eastern quarter of the country, and even further afield, but they are probably still most numerous in the Wealden district.

The Wealden house forms a simple rectangle on the ground floor and consists of a central hall, open to the roof and containing an open hearth, with two-storey portions at each end, one with service rooms on the ground floor, the other with private rooms, both with chambers up above. Entrance was by way of a cross-passage at the 'lower' or service end of the hall. The similarity with the medieval Large House will be obvious though these houses were on a smaller scale. The really distinctive feature of the Wealden house is its arrangement on the upper floor, for it was customary to project, or 'jetty', the chambers in each wing towards the front, making a very flat U on the first floor over the rectangular ground floor plan. The roof, which was usually a hipped roof or gablet-type roof, reverted to the rectangular shape; the wall plate between the two jettied storeys was supported by curved braces at the angles and there was a deep eaves at this central length.

It is therefore very easy to recognise a Wealden house from the outside. One simply looks for evidence of the central hall, the jettied upper floors of the token wings, and the deep eaves in between. Wealden houses normally have very steeply pitched roofs designed for thatch or plain tiles, and this great expanse of tile, as it usually is nowadays, hipped back towards a short ridge, ties in the rather intricate arrangement below and gives an air of stability, even serenity to such houses. There are houses which have the same general arrangement but lack the projecting upper floors, there are others in which the chambers project on three sides. In the towns one may find houses of standard Wealden arrangement but also the so-called 'Half-Wealden' was used on narrow sites, there being only one jettied chamber floor and so only one token cross-wing.

Wealden houses were built for prosperous farmers and others of similar social standing from the fourteenth to the early sixteenth century. Few remain unaltered, the most common improvement having been the insertion of an intermediate floor in the hall, forming a new chamber lit from a dormer window, and the introduction of a fireplace actually blocking the cross-passage and rising to a prominent and highly decorated brick chimney stack. These improvements mark the late sixteenth–late seventeenth century period. Rather later, during the eighteenth and early nineteenth centuries, many such houses were modernised by having a new outer wall of brick or tile applied on the line of the jettied chamber floor.

Is it a cross-passage house?

The idea of having a cross-passage as the means of entering a house seems to have become well-established during the Middle Ages and persisted into the seventeenth century when so many of our surviving Small Houses were built. There are several types and sub-types in which this feature may be seen. They have in common not only the cross-passage itself but also the fact that the main hearth or fireplace, the one serving the kitchen/living room, backs onto the cross-passage: to get into the principal room one has to go into the cross-passage and then along the side of the fireplace or the inglenook around the hearth.

The arrangement may be detected from outside the building by the relative positions of the main chimney stack and the main entrance door. If a line from this stack falls just to one side of the doorway jamb then the position of the cross-passage is indicated. Often the fireplace or inglenook is located towards the front of the building and lit by a small so-called 'fire-window'. In such a case we have a further clue to the arrangement, and we can also see that to reach the main room one has to go right round the seat of the fire.

The simplest, and generally the earliest type of cross-passage house, is that which has a kitchen/living room and an inner private room to one side of the cross-passage and either a service room or a cow-house to the other side. In either case the main room would be open to the roof and the inner room similarly open or given a ceiling so as to provide a loft for storage or sleeping. Where there is a cow-house beyond the cross-passage we have the arrangement which has been given the name 'longhouse'. The tradition of keeping the valuable cattle—oxen for ploughing or cows for milking—under the same roof as the farmer and his family is a very old-established one, and the role of the cross-passage providing both common access and a sort of social separation between animals and humans is one full of significance. Both variations of the

25. House at Blencarn, Westmorland (now Cumbria)
This farmhouse retains the cross-passage which formerly gave access both to the house and the cow-house. The farm building portion on the left retains the low eaves and steeply pitched roof of the original thatch; the domestic portion on the right has been raised or rebuilt to give two comfortable storeys under a low-pitched roof of slate.

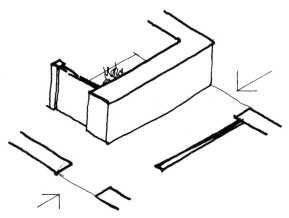

a. Hearth backing onto cross-passage

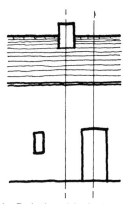

b. Relationship between doorway and chimney

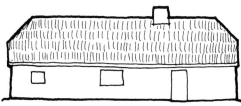

c. Three units, one heated

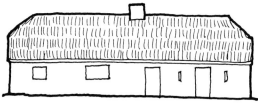

d. Two units plus cow-house (a long house)

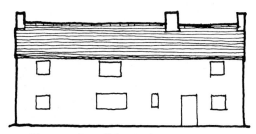

e. Three units, all heated

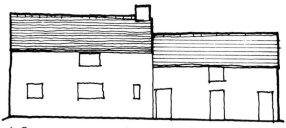

f. Cross-passage made when adding a cow-house

h. Late survival of cross-passage

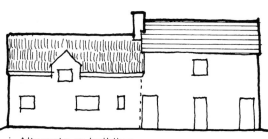

i. Alternate re-building

50

basic cross-passage plan have long, low proportions with low eaves and a great expanse of roof.

Development of this house-plan included the general up-grading of accommodation. The loft became a continuous bedroom floor; the unheated inner room and service room became heated parlours and kitchens. Such houses with low rooms and smoky interiors became tall well-proportioned elevations enlivened by the chimney stacks of lots of fireplaces, and were still being erected until early in the nineteenth century. Development also took another direction, that of alternate rebuilding, in which first the part for the humans and then the part for the animals was rebuilt, a change of material or roof-line indicating the sequence. There was one other variation whereby the plan was a result of accretion: a cow-house attached by a cross-passage to an earlier house.

Is it a baffle-entry house?

While the cross-passage as a means of entry into a house is old-established, access against the jamb of a fireplace or inglenook enclosure is at least as common. The cross-passage itself provides an oddly inconvenient way of getting into a building but entry into a small lobby against the jamb is hardly less so: the one almost ensures a draughty approach, the other almost ensures that one door is going to get in the way of another. It may be that the baffle-entry developed from the cross-passage because, as we have seen, one of the developments of the Wealden House plan entailed blocking a cross-passage by

26. Is it a cross-passage house?

27. House at Great Barrington, Cambridgeshire
The disposition of the windows and the relationship between the chimney stack and the doorway show this to be a baffle-entry house.

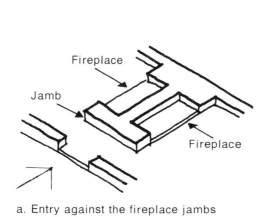

a. Entry against the fireplace jambs

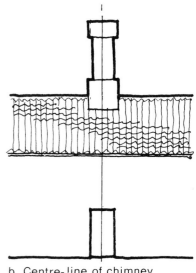

b. Centre-line of chimney falls within doorway

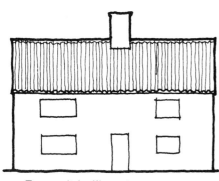

c. Two-unit baffle-entry

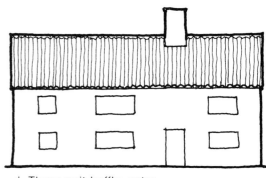

d. Three-unit baffle-entry

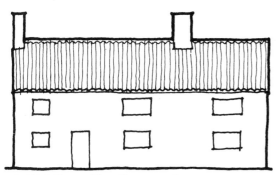

e. Variation with entry away from back-to-back fireplaces

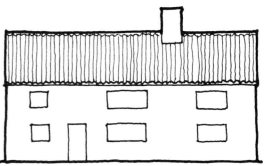

f. As e., but with only two heated rooms

the insertion of a fireplace whose jamb walls then opposed the entrance door. But many houses from the late sixteenth and early seventeenth century onwards were erected on this pattern.

The baffle-entry house plan may easily be recognised from the outside. If one draws an imaginary line down from the principal chimney stack and it falls within the width of the front doorway then the plan has been used. The centre-line of the stack does not always coincide with that of the doorway because sometimes an extra hearth has been placed back-to-back with an older one, but the line will not pass outside the doorway jamb as is always the case where there is a cross-passage. The massive chimney stack is also characteristic: it rises from part way along the ridge then usually forms a base for separate stacks, each flue serving a single fireplace until they unite again with a chimney cap which is often highly decorated.

Some houses of this plan have two living units on each floor, others have three. In the former pattern there is a kitchen/living room to one side of the entrance lobby and fireplace stack and a heated parlour to the other side; the arrangement is rarely completely symmetrical because the kitchen/living room and its chamber are normally wider than parlour and parlour chamber. The other pattern has kitchen/living room and parlour to one side of the entrance and kitchen or heated parlour to the other side. Both plans developed particularly well in East Anglia during the seventeenth century and the baffle-entry arrangement crossed the Atlantic with the colonists and formed the basis for one strand in the web of American vernacular architecture.

There is one plan which seems to be related to the others in that the main fireplaces are back to back but the entrance is into the living room near where it joins the unheated parlour or other inner room. Strictly speaking this is not a baffle-entry plan; it may result from the conflict in the designer's mind between the wish to place the front door in what had become a traditional position and the wish to be more up-to-date and put the door nearer the centre of the main room on the elevation.

Is it a double-pile Small House?

The culmination of vernacular house planning at the Large House level in the late seventeenth century was the so-called 'double-pile' house and this plan was the culmination about a century later of vernacular planning at the Small House level. The double-pile plan takes its name from the characteristic use of two rooms throughout the depth of the house at each floor level, and as a consequence of this and the use of tall rooms on two or more storeys houses of this plan take a solid cubic shape as they stand four-square in town, village or farmstead.

The standard arrangement is to have living room and parlour on the front and kitchen and dairy or scullery on the rear with the staircase between them. On the first floor there would be four bedrooms corresponding to the four rooms below. Often there was an attic or garret in the roof space and sometimes there was a cellar under at least part of the ground floor. Entrance was from the front into one corner of the living room and there was a back door into the kitchen as well. All rooms except the dairy were usually heated and fireplaces were usually located in the side walls, though in one major variation the fireplaces were

28. Is it a baffle-entry house?

29. House in Keswick, Cumberland (now Cumbria)

This double-pile house represents the culmination of vernacular domestic house planning in that part of the country; at the front there are a few fashionable architectural details but the cobble and slate-stone walls and the sandstone dressings place the building firmly in its locality. Even in the photograph the deep roof may be seen as covering two rooms from front to back.

located back-to-back in the centre of the plan on the partition walls between front and back rooms.

The double-pile plan is easily recognised from the outside by its deep plan, cubic form, and neat arrangement of windows and doors—and usually other architectural details—quite formally patterned under Renaissance influence. Curiously enough, Small Houses of this plan are rarely symmetrical on the front elevation. Instead the front door is pushed rather to one side so as to give a reasonable width to the parlour on the front; this can rarely be detected at first glance except that in the very smallest examples the door is pushed considerably to one side. It is also curious that what we would regard as the elementary improvement to the plan provided by the introduction of a passage between front door and staircase occurred so infrequently and so late at the Small House level. Where buildings were designed with this convenience then there would be a fanlight over the front door to light the passage.

Although it is easy to see the double-pile Small House as an imitation on a smaller scale of the same plan at the Large House level it can also be seen as the culmination of a process of extension. Thus we have house plans extended at the rear, first at ground floor level with the main roof swept down in a 'catslide', then at first floor level too, but with an eaves lower at the rear than at the front, and finally made into the conventional form.

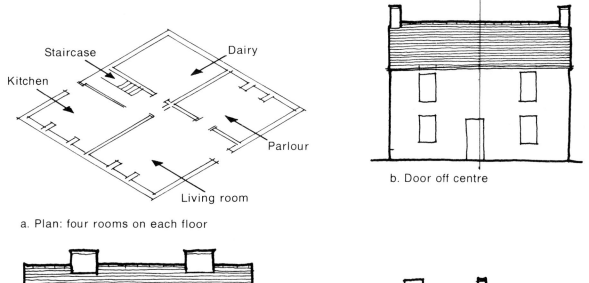

Staircase

Kitchen

Dairy

Parlour

Living room

a. Plan: four rooms on each floor

b. Door off centre

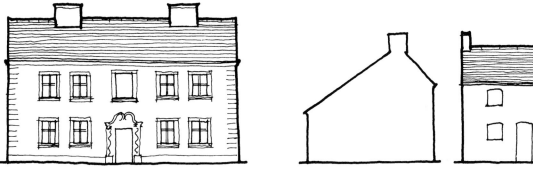

c. The Large House predecessor

d. The outshut predecessor

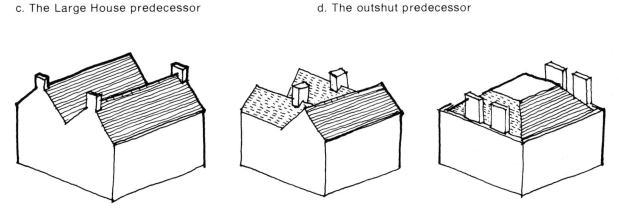

e. Parallel roofs over the plan

f. Rear rooms roofed as wings

g. Flat-topped pyramid roof

**30. Is it a double-pile
Small House?**

The problem of roofing these unusually deep buildings deserves mention. Where a material such as stone flag or slate could be used at a low pitch the problem was not severe but other materials and sleeper pitches led to all sorts of expedients to preserve a neat appearance at the front.

Is it a single-fronted cottage?

Of the several types of cottage which can be seen in town and countryside the one which is the most numerous, though not, perhaps, the one which springs immediately to mind, is the single-fronted cottage in its several versions. The estate agents' term 'single-fronted' provides a convenient label because the cottages are of asymmetrical shape in themselves, presenting one (or sometimes two) windows and a door on the front elevation, marking a single room on the front of the building.

Early and miniature cottages of this description have only one room effectively: the front door opens into a single room containing a hearth and housing all domestic activities, except that most of the surviving examples have

31. Cottages at Tattingstone, Suffolk
The chimney stacks and dormer windows indicate that this was originally built as a row of four cottages though some windows and doors have been re-positioned. Each cottage would have had one main room on the ground floor and the one other room in the roof space.

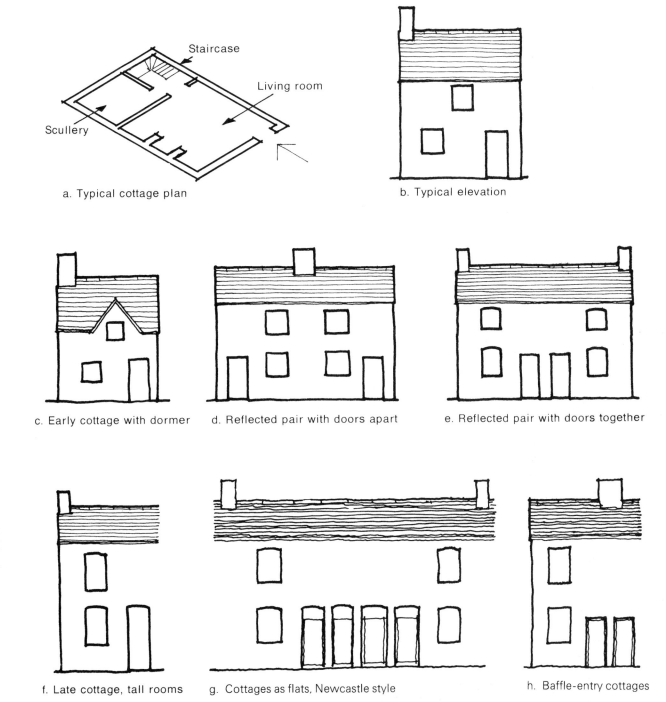

a. Typical cottage plan

Staircase

Living room

Scullery

b. Typical elevation

c. Early cottage with dormer

d. Reflected pair with doors apart

e. Reflected pair with doors together

f. Late cottage, tall rooms

g. Cottages as flats, Newcastle style

h. Baffle-entry cottages

32. Is it a single-fronted cottage?

a loft or room in the roof space, reached by a ladder or very steep and narrow staircase, and capable of serving as a bedroom. Later cottages have a full-height room on each floor. All these cottages are very shallow from front to back; the earliest and smallest ones are very low with the loft space lit by a small window in a gable, under a half-hip, in a dormer at the front or half hidden by the eaves; later ones have an upstairs window squeezed practically to floor level; all have a chimney stack which seems out of proportion to such a tiny dwelling.

Rather later and superior versions of the single-fronted cottage had an extra room and a staircase at the rear. The extra room served as a scullery or dairy; it was rarely heated. The staircase was usually a tight winding staircase giving much improved access to a first floor containing one substantial bedroom and another much smaller. The earlier and smaller cottages were sometimes found singly, sometimes in sets of two or three, and, in towns especially, may be found in long rows extending down the depth of a long narrow plot. It was this plan which formed the basis for the much maligned 'back-to-back'* houses which have now been almost completely cleared away from our cities. The later and superior cottages were often built as pairs with some serious attempt at symmetry either by means of grouped chimney stacks or grouped doorways. Both in town and countryside these can still be seen as charming and well-proportioned little buildings.

The latest cottages which fall within the vernacular province are those with four main rooms. Their common name 'two-up and two-down' gives a perfect description since they had on the ground floor a kitchen/living room and a scullery/wash-house, and had two bedrooms on the upper floor. All rooms had fireplaces. Internally they differed on the placing of the staircase but externally all were basically the same in the placing of the two windows and a door. The rhythm of these elements mars or graces many of our city streets according to one's point of view!

Farm buildings

What applies to domestic buildings applies to some extent to the other buildings of the farmstead. Here, again, design relates primarily to function, tradition and fashion, and then to available building materials. Once more, certain broad tendencies may be distinguished.

Obviously most of the farmer's work is done out in the open in the fields, but in the climate enjoyed or endured by farmers in this country certain activities involving the sheltering and tending of stock and the storage and processing of crops are better done under cover than in the open. There was a tendency, therefore, for farm building to increase in number and size as more and more such activities were conducted under cover. Excavation suggest that the typical medieval farmstead consisted of one building which houses humans and oxen, and another, much smaller, which housed the crops. The oldest surviving farm buildings are the great medieval tithe barns, intended for the richest clients, and used, in any case, for the special purpose of accommodating crops

* Such true 'back-to-back' houses had only one exposure; even in Leeds and Bradford their numbers are much reduced.

taken as taxes paid in kind, or the produce of farms which were exceptionally large and productive. But their survival tends to obscure the fact that contemporary farm buildings were few and flimsy and that substantial farm buildings tend to be late and, on the smallest farms, very late indeed. As farming became more efficient and more capital-intensive so more animals were housed, more crops housed and more and more processes done under cover.

There was a tendency for most buildings to be designed for increasingly specialised functions. The corn barn (sometimes separate corn barns for different types of cereal), the hay barn, the cow-house, the stable (usually separate stables for different grades of horse), the cart shed, the granary, the shelter shed, the pig sty, the dovecot, the poultry house, the ash-house, the drying kiln, and, later the mixing room and the cooling house all came to be provided as separate recognisable buildings or parts of buildings. Many family farms had one of each of the buildings listed, larger farms might have several.

Another tendency was for the greater number of buildings to be arranged to form a farmyard serving as a hub for the newly-housed activities. One important function for the farmyard was to provide a central storage point for the accumulation of manure, itself one of the most valuable products of agriculture in the days before artificial fertilisers were available. Another function was the enclosure of young cattle running loose and treading down the manure. In some cases the yard was even covered, the better to protect cattle and manure from the weather.

The arrangement of farm buildings in relation to the fields, the land slope, the water supply, the yard and to each other became increasingly affected by the need for labour economy, especially in those parts of the country in which mines and quarries, factories and furnaces provided tempting alternative employment for the mid-eighteenth century labourer. One can see the result in the design of buildings in which gravity took fodder down to animals and manure down to middens and in the eventual use of connecting buildings with tramways linking the central mixing plant to the cattle stalls.

There was a further tendency towards the multiplication of satellite farm buildings: outfarms, each one containing a barn, a cow-house, a stable, and a shelter shed but with at most a labourer's cottage by way of domestic accommodation; field barns with accommodation for hay and cattle or sheep. These satellites reflected the expansion of cultivated land in the century ending in about 1880.

The largest farmsteads received the benefit of design by architects specialising in farm buildings and working under the influence of the agricultural theorists especially in the nineteenth century. They were often show-places, often extravagant, often uneconomical and sometimes they bankrupted their sponsors. They were the equivalent among farm buildings to the 'polite' works in domestic architecture. But they were vastly outnumbered by the farmsteads of family farms, examples of vernacular architecture varying with the type of farming conducted, the status of the farmer, the time of construction and in the use of what building materials were available. These form an essential component in the patchwork of the British countryside. A few selected examples are covered in more detail as encouragement towards a deeper study of these buildings while they still remain.

33. Court Farm Barn
from Lee-on-Solent,
Hampshire
Re-erected at the Weald
and Downland Open Air
Museum this timber-
framed barn was
probably first built in the
late seventeenth or early
eighteenth century. The
aisles extend along two
sides and continue along
one end.

Is it an aisled barn?

The standard barn of England and Wales consists of three parts: a central threshing floor and cartway and storage bays on each side. In the smaller versions these correspond to three structural divisions or bays, in the larger versions the storage areas are correspondingly larger and take two structural bays each while the threshing floor still occupies one. In some later versions there is a larger storage unit on one side of the threshing floor than the other. In some still larger versions there are two threshing floors with various arrangements for storage on each side and between. In all cases the basic core of the barn is revealed externally by the pattern of large barn door and more or less blank walls to the storage bays.

One important version of what the Americans call the English Barn is the aisled barn. As the name suggests the aisled barn is arranged rather like a church with a tall central nave and lower side aisles: sometimes there is only one aisle though usually there are two. Normally the roof sweeps down from the ridge over both nave and aisles, but there is no clerestory lighting the nave as in so many churches. Internally the aisled barns are usually quite grand as they have the strong rhythm of the lines of posts supporting intricate roof trusses within the dark heights of the roof space, and also the arrangement of braces in each direction gives something of the effect of the arcading in a church interior. However there is a fundamental difference between the organisation of an aisled church and an aisled barn. The church is arranged according to its long axis, running east and west and taking the eye from the extremities of the nave at the west to the culmination in the altar at the east; the barn is arranged as a barn

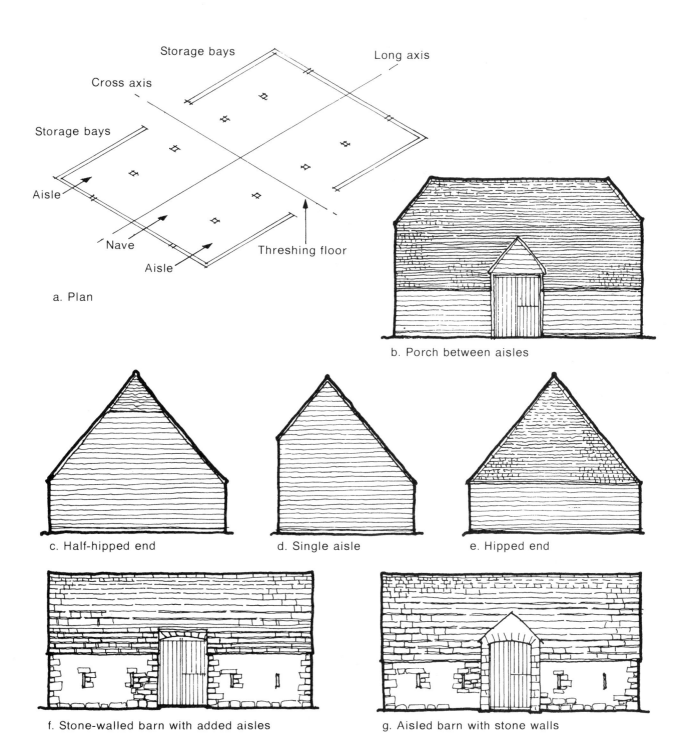

Storage bays

Cross axis

Storage bays

Aisle

Nave

Aisle

Long axis

Threshing floor

a. Plan

b. Porch between aisles

c. Half-hipped end

d. Single aisle

e. Hipped end

f. Stone-walled barn with added aisles

g. Aisled barn with stone walls

34. Is it an aisled barn?

61

should be with the threshing bay in the centre and storage bays at each side—in architectural terms there is a strong cross-axis to balance the longitudinal axis.

Usually the threshing floor is extended, at least towards the farmyard, by means of a porch running between or beyond the aisle; sometimes the barn doors are set back between the aisles. The most easily recognisable aisled barns are those of the southern and eastern counties which are completely timber-framed and have a cladding of weatherboard, but other materials have been used, and the Yorkshire Pennines, for instance, are full of aisled barns with stone walls and stone flagged roofs very solid in appearance and hiding quite graceful interiors. In the North of England one may see aisled barns which have resulted from a process of accretion, since the demand for milk in areas becoming industrialised encouraged farmers to add cow-houses to their barns in the form of aisles.

Is it a granary?

Until quite recently, virtually all farms were mixed farms in that grain crops had to be grown to feed the family, to provide a small cash surplus for paying the rent, and to help feed the animals during the winter, while animals had to be kept for food, for sale and to provide manure. Again, until about two hundred

35. Granary at Peper Harow, Surrey
This unusually large granary was probably built early in the seventeenth century. It is timber-framed and has a plain tiled roof and tile cladding to the upper storeys. The open bays on the ground floor still serve as an implement shed.

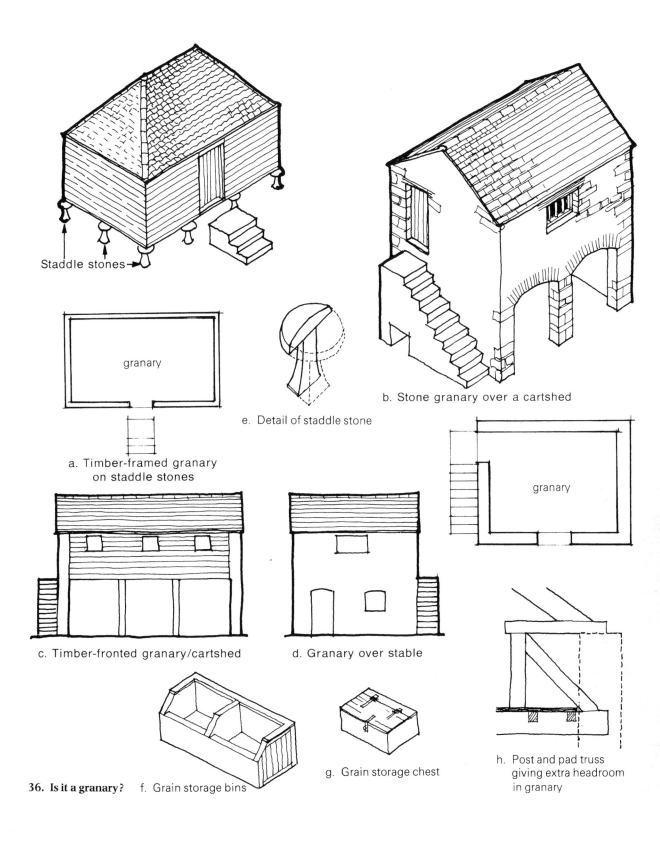

Staddle stones

granary

a. Timber-framed granary on staddle stones

e. Detail of staddle stone

b. Stone granary over a cartshed

granary

c. Timber-fronted granary/cartshed

d. Granary over stable

h. Post and pad truss giving extra headroom in granary

36. Is it a granary?   f. Grain storage bins

g. Grain storage chest

63

years ago, yields of grain crops were so poor that they were consumed or sold practically as they were harvested. When each grain of wheat sowed could only produce a threefold or up to fivefold increase even in a good year, and one grain had to be kept back for sowing to produce next year's crop, the surplus was very small indeed. At this time such corn as had to be stored was kept in the house; in the loft or even in the parlour in conditions which provided freedom from damp, freedom from rats and security against robbery. Only the very largest establishments had any need for a granary as such.

When, as part of the successive agricultural revolutions, productivity improved tremendously, it was necessary to provide a specialised building to act as granary, both so that the larger amounts of grain used on the farm could be stored, and so that grain for sale could be kept as long as possible—even from year to year—so as to secure the best price. Two types of granary were devised. In one the grain was kept in chests, sacks or loose on the floor of a small timber-framed building raised on staddle stones to provide ventilation and as protection from rats; the building was usually clad in weatherboard or hung with slates or tiles to ensure good protection from the rain but also adequate ventilation. In the other type, the granary proper was raised to first floor level over an open-fronted structure which served as a cartshed. There was a staircase (often an external staircase), giving access to the granary, and as domestic-type windows were used for light and ventilation and good quality construction and materials generally were used, such a granary sometimes looks like a domestic flat over the open-fronted ground floor.

On the larger farms the granaries were correspondingly large and elaborate, being arranged on two upper floors, in some cases, so as to accommodate the grain produced in exceptionally good years. On the smaller farms granaries are often associated with the farmhouse, being an extension of the main farmhouse building and even intercommunicating with the bedrooms. On other farms the granary was sometimes placed over the stable for convenience since the horses consumed lots of oats and, one imagines, as a further token of the high regard which horses enjoyed over other farm animals.

Is it a field barn?

No-one who has visited the Yorkshire Dales can fail to have noticed the field barns which form such an essential part of the landscape and a major part of the vernacular architecture of the county. As the valleys narrow into their Pennine origins so more and more of these isolated structures come to the eye until practically every field seems to possess its own field barn. What applies to the Yorkshire Dales applies to some extent to many of the upland areas in the country and field barns are also prominent in Derbyshire and Caernarvonshire, for instance.

The purpose of a field barn is to provide storage for hay and accommodation for cattle consuming the hay in the winter. The provision of a field barn eliminates the need to cart hay to the farmstead in the autumn and manure back to the fields during the spring; instead young cattle, at least, can be tethered or run in loose boxes, eating up the hay and treading down the manure and needing only a daily visit for watering, foddering and exercise. Sometimes milking cattle were kept in field barns, when the daily visit included milking and

37. Field barns at Thwaite, Swaledale, Yorkshire, N.R.
These barns, satellites of distant farmsteads, accommodated cattle and hay for their winter fodder. The buildings are in typical locations, each in the middle of a field or at the boundary between smaller fields. The boldly projecting 'through stones' are characteristic of field barns in the dale.

bringing the milk down to the dairy in a back pack churn. Sometimes oats or rye were grown in the upper fields and threshed day by day in the field barn. Generally, the scattering of field barns, on newly enclosed and cultivated land, contrasts with the villages and hamlets tightly congested in the valley bottoms within the ring of former open fields.

The field barns may be recognised first by their location, secondly by their siting and thirdly by their form. In location they are, of course, distant from the farm (though some of the larger ones are in fact quite near to the farmstead but well outside the farmstead group) and are placed either in the middle of a field, in one corner, or at one side; each location enables hay to be swept from upper slopes and manure to be readily spread on lower slopes. In siting they are usually built into a rise in the ground so that the crops can be put easily into the upper level and the animals brought into the ground level. In form the siting plays a big part: those end on to the slope have the pitching eye for crops in the upper gable and the door to the cow-house or loose box in a lower side wall. Often there is a loft above the cow-house but a deep haymow alongside, giving great storage capacity; those side on to the slope can have greater space for animals, or a convenient arrangement for bringing hay out at the lower level, to feed to sheltering sheep, for instance. Not all field barns are on a slope or high in the valleys and, in Derbyshire and Staffordshire especially, many are on the lower land, have less space for internal storage of crops and more space for tethered cattle.

a. Field barn end on to slope

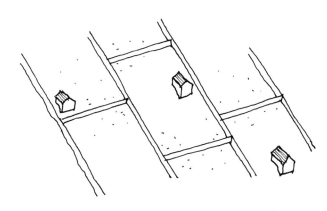

b. Various positions for field barns

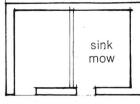

sink
mow

c. Plan

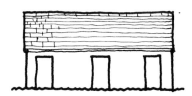

d. Midland-type field cowhouse

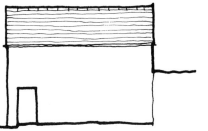

e. Field barn side on to slope

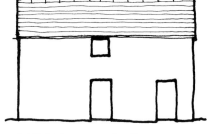

f. Field barn on the flat

38. Is it a field barn?

Other vernacular buildings

As in domestic and farm buildings so in minor industrial buildings and other vernacular buildings certain broad trends can be detected which linked function, tradition and fashion in building form. The earliest examples showed traditional responses to what were essentially traditional activities conducted on a larger scale than before; the latest examples showed that a professional hand was required in designing for an entirely new activity or one conducted on an entirely new scale. In most cases the processes required more and bigger buildings showing greater and greater specialisation.

As they were basically utilitarian buildings there was a close connection between the process and the form of the minor industrial buildings, and, where power was required, as it usually was, between the form and the power source. Thus we can see that various textile operations involving relatively small, lightweight and simple machinery graduated only from the house to the backyard workshop as long as human muscle provided the power. As larger and heavier machines were invented either horse power or, more commonly, water power was harnessed. Such power sources were best used to drive machines linked by belts and shafts of limited length and so the multi-storey textile mill was devised. When steam replaced water the same method of distribution of power was used and the same general appearance was maintained.

Of the range of minor industrial building types, two have been selected for some further consideration. Windmills and watermills have a long history as vernacular building types; even the very latest of such buildings hardly stepped towards polite architecture. For other types there was a compressed development from initiation, as adaptations of related building types, to full professional design and specialist construction in no more than a couple of generations. All types are represented by a rapidly dwindling number of examples as even more swift industrial developments require that processes and buildings are devised and superseded within less than a lifetime.

What sort of a windmill?

We sometimes forget that energy shortage has been a more or less permanent state for mankind and that our ancestors were just as concerned to find energy from sources free from the need to bear, rear and feed cattle or horses or humans as we are to discover energy sources which are not finite, will not be subject to commercial blackmail and will be free from pollution. One relatively cheap method of obtaining energy in favourable circumstances was to harness the winds to drive windmills.

Such mills or machines were mainly used for grinding corn, but were also used for pumping drainage water from level to level and sometimes for driving machinery in farms or even factories. Windmills for grinding corn were usually sited on hilltops, near the villages but where the wind could best be caught. Drainage windmills were tied to the drainage channels but were on flat land where winds blew unobstructed. Windmills for driving machinery were much more rare but when found are seen to rise from the top of the buildings housing the machinery.

There are two main types of free-standing windmill and one important

39. Windmill at Great Chishill, Hertfordshire
This timber-framed post mill has a very attractive cladding of white-painted weather-boarding.

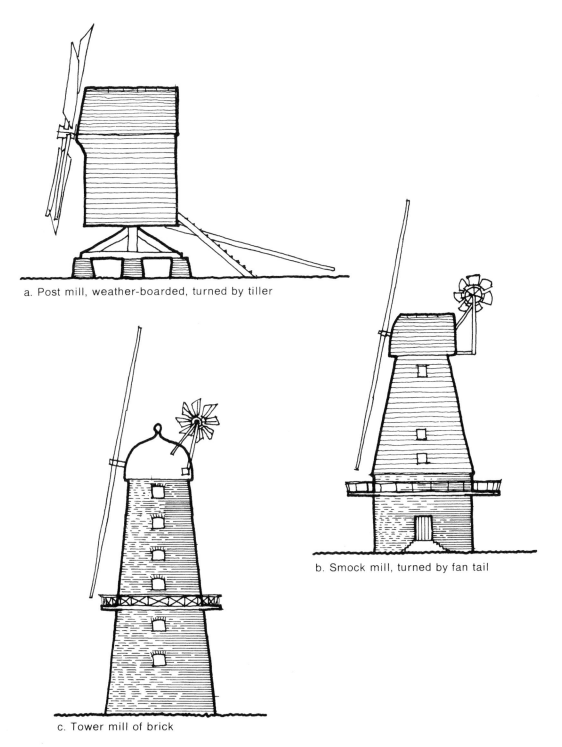

a. Post mill, weather-boarded, turned by tiller

b. Smock mill, turned by fan tail

c. Tower mill of brick

40. What sort of a windmill?

41. Windmill at Rolvenden, Kent
This smock mill was built probably in the late seventeenth or early eighteenth century though it has been restored since then. The four sweeps and the tailpiece help make a dramatic feature in the landscape.

42. Windmill at Skidby, Yorkshire, E.R.
The brick tower mill rises from a set of brick farm and industrial buildings. A fantail turns the cap and its sails into the wind while a balcony near the base of the tower allows access to the sails.

subsidiary: the post mill, the tower mill and its subsidiary the smock mill. In the post mill the sails are attached to shafting and gear wheels and ultimately to grindstones or pump in a superstructure which turns on a post into the wind. In the tower mill the sails and shafting and some of the gears are in a rotating cap, but the rest of the equipment is in a tall brick or stone tower which can raise the cap and sails far higher into the wind than was possible with the post mill. In the smock mill the arrangement is basically as in a tower mill, but the tower is timber-framed rather than solid walled.

There were three main ways in which the sails could be kept in the best position in relation to an ever-changing wind direction: by turning a pole, by rotating with the aid of pulley and chain from a gallery, and automatically with the aid of a fantail. Each way affected the appearance of the windmill. In the first system a long projecting pole had to be lifted or wheeled about a circular track — this system was used for post mills; in the second a gallery part way up the tower or smock allowed the miller to operate a relatively short length of chain; in the third a small set of sails at right angles to the main sails operated gearing which kept the main sails in the best possible position.

Quite a number of windmills survive, and in recent years several have been renovated in most of the counties where they were once common. But even the stump or framework of a long abandoned mill can tell the observant traveller something about its original arrangement.

What sort of a watermill?
The energy stored in falling water provided an alternative and more reliable source of power than that harnessed by the windmill, and watermills have been used even longer than windmills. Until the Industrial Revolution most watermills were for grinding corn but some were for fulling woollen cloth and others provided power for bellows or simple machinery. During the Industrial Revolution these uses continued but to them were added the supply of power for textile and other machinery, and for bellows at furnaces and also for pumping in mines. Watermills were located either on the upper reaches of streams, using the energy stored in relatively small amounts of swiftly flowing water, or on the lower reaches of rivers utilising the energy in the large quantities of slowly moving water; a few watermills were on the coast, harnessing the energy stored in sea water which could be trapped at high tide and gradually allowed to escape turning the water wheel at low tide. There were two main ways of bringing the water to the wheel: below the mill, turning a horizontal wheel in the form known as a 'click mill' — of ancient invention but still to be found in the Scottish Islands; and alongside the mill, with water led to the top, the bottom, or halfway up the wheel. Some mills, both for grinding and machinery power, had internal water wheels; later mills were constructed or adapted to make use of the more efficient turbines.

The appearance of the vernacular watermill varied with its siting, its distribution of harnessed power, and with the materials and constructional methods used. The lowland mill was on a flat site on the river bank, was three storeys in height throughout, and usually was built either of timber-frame or brick. The highland mill was built into a slope, near a natural or artificial dam or weir, and was three storeys in height above the lower level, but only two at the

43. Watermill at King's Cliffe, Northamptonshire
This water-powered mill stands right beside the river near the middle of the little town. The characteristic three storeys can be seen; they accommodate machinery, millstones and grain stores respectively.

upper and usually built of stone. In all cases it was normal to have a lowest level containing the shaft from the mill wheel and its attendant gearing, an intermediate level containing the millstones and an upper level (which might be partly in the roof space) containing the store for the unmilled grain. Attached to the mill of upland location there was very often a kiln, a platform on which damp grain could be dried by warm air from a charcoal furnace; this kiln was concealed within the walls and rarely had the moveable cowl one associates with the generally similar oasthouse. Very often there was a cartshed, stable and hayloft for the miller's horse and cart as a further appendage to the main mill building.

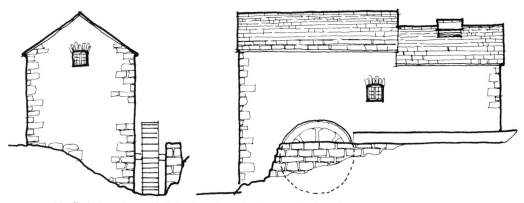

a. and b. End elevation and side elevation of mill on a sloping site

c. Half-timbered mill

d. Timber-frame and weather-board mill on a flat site

e. Brick-walled mill on a flat site

f. 'Click mill' as surviving in northern Scotland

Few watermills now survive intact though there has been a welcome move to restore good examples to their original use or convert them to other uses, but practically every watercourse bears the remains or ruins of the incredible number of mills which once used the energy stored in falling water over and over again.

What sort of a chapel?

All but a few of the Anglican parish churches were examples of polite architecture and, of course, many rank very high on the scale of architectural quality. The religious fervour of the nineteenth century saw the construction of huge numbers of church buildings for Anglicans. Non-Conformists and Roman Catholics and these, too, are generally accepted as works of polite architecture though of varying standards. But there was a period from the late seventeenth century to the early nineteenth century in which most Non-Conformists and some Anglicans worshipped in humble, unpretentious buildings fully deserving to be classified as examples of vernacular architecture.

Although there had been congregations of Dissenters from the Established Church meeting since the middle of the sixteenth century it was not until after the Toleration Act of 1689 had been passed that the congregations felt able to erect meeting-houses in any numbers. Then the numbers were very substantial and it has been estimated that practically 2,500 chapels and meeting-houses were erected before 1700. This great burst of construction coincided with the

44. What sort of watermill?

45. Friends' Meeting House, Pardshaw, Dean, Cumberland
The building was erected in 1729; the original entrance was in the middle of the elevation. Built of whitewashed local stone and with a roof of thick slates this chapel is as much a part of the vernacular architecture of its locality as the nearby houses and cottages.

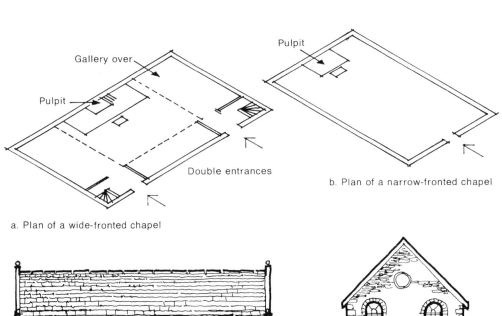

Gallery over

Pulpit

Double entrances

a. Plan of a wide-fronted chapel

Pulpit

b. Plan of a narrow-fronted chapel

c. Late 17C Unitarian chapel

d. 19C Methodist chapel

e. 17C chapel with shelter for horses

f. 17C Quaker Meeting House, cottage alongside

g. 19C Methodist chapel with keeper's cottage

h. 17C Baptist chapel

similar burst of rebuilding and new construction of houses, especially in those counties in which the Non-Conformist sects were strong. Their use of local materials and adaptation of traditional forms meant that the buildings were unobtrusive in communities which might be suspicious of the new forms of worship; architecturally the buildings took their place among the cottages and farmhouses of the village and did not compete with the church on the hill.

The outward appearance of the chapel or meeting-house reflects its internal organisation as closely as that of a farmhouse or barn. The Quaker meeting-houses were the simplest: a service without liturgy and without formal preaching required only a single bare room, having a committee room and a gallery partitioned off one end, a single door and a few domestic-scaled windows. Chapels for Unitarians or Congregationalists were little more complicated: there was a single tall meeting room dominated by a pulpit on one long side and with galleries at both ends, sometimes joined opposite the pulpit; externally the long entrance side had two doors, two tall windows and two staircases outside or two windows lighting internal staircases. The 'Village Bethels' of the nineteenth century Methodists had a pulpit at one end, a gallery at the other and an entrance and flanking staircases under the gallery and through the gable. Many chapels and meeting-houses had a cottage attached for the caretaker, and those serving a scattered congregation had a stable or shelter for the horses.

Building materials were those of the locality and the time—brick in East Anglia, gritstone in the Pennines, rendered limestone in Westmorland and black slate-like stones in Wales.

46. What sort of chapel?

Chapter 5

What are the common walling and roofing methods and materials?

As an introduction to vernacular architecture we have been looking at siting, function, plan and section because that is the way one assumes the original builders looked at their architectural problems, but as observers seeking to note, understand and appreciate the buildings around us, we tend to see the building first and its plan and section later (if at all): the bricks or stone, tiles or thatch, and then that disposition of doors and windows, floor levels and chimney stacks which reveals the plan.

A considerable variety of building materials has been available to the designers of vernacular buildings in this country. The land provided stone of all sorts, it provided clay and timber and could be made to supply the ingredients for bricks and tiles and crops for thatch. As building materials are so heavy and expensive to move it has, until recently, been customary to use the materials which were immediately to hand for all except the most important buildings, such as cathedrals and palaces and other monumental works. But often there is more than one material to hand—timber above stone, and straw for thatch being reaped from clay lands suitable for tile making. So it seems that the choice of material actually to be used depended on a balance between tradition and fashion as well as between economy and extravagant display.

The constructional basis for vernacular architecture has been, as it continues to be for virtually all buildings, either frame or mass. In frame construction the loads of roof and intermediate floors are conducted through the separate vertical elements of the frame safely to the foundations and so to the ground. The wall fabric serves as the enclosing element, keeping out rain and cold, keeping in heat, maintaining privacy. Except insofar as elements of the frame may also be elements of the wall the whole fabric could be eliminated and the wall would still subsist; indeed the actual constructional process is usually a matter of frame first, wall fabric last. In mass construction the loads of roof and intermediate floors are conducted through the wall to a foundation which thus carries both wall loads and the superimposed loads. Without the wall, the roof and floors could not be carried; the wall is built first, floor and roof construction follows. These points may seem obvious enough but it is all too easy to become fascinated by carpentry joints and bricklayer's tricks and forget that the two trades represent entirely different attitudes to structural problems.

In vernacular architecture, frame construction has depended almost entirely on the use of timber. In so-called box-frame construction the structural members also formed part of the wall; in what we have come to call cruck construction the structural members were usually concealed and the wall could be of any material—including timber-frame. Mass wall construction has depended on the use of stone (which includes flint, cobbles and pebbles), of brick

47. Houses at Weobley, Herefordshire

The two main techniques of timber-framed construction; to the right is a house with cruck trusses visible in the gable and with walls of square panels in half-timber; to the left are houses of box-frame construction, but upper storeys are jettied.

and of clay or earth in various guises. In general it seems that timber-frame construction was the normal constructional method for vernacular architecture over virtually the whole country and persisted in some parts until the extinction of vernacular building within the past century; stone succeeded timber-frame for humble buildings wherever it was at hand, remaining in use again until the late nineteenth century; brick was introduced for special purposes, such as for fireplaces and chimneys, in the sixteenth century and has been widely used since the mid-seventeenth century; clay and earth have proved to be of very long-standing use, and, again, persisted in certain parts of the country as elements in the vernacular builder's repertoire until well into the nineteenth century.

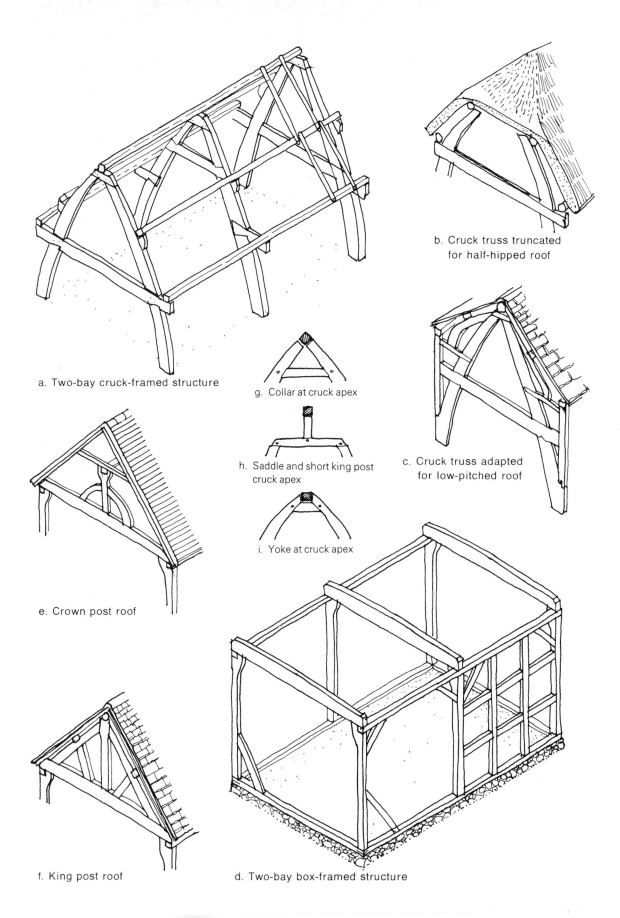

b. Cruck truss truncated
for half-hipped roof

a. Two-bay cruck-framed structure

g. Collar at cruck apex

h. Saddle and short king post
cruck apex

i. Yoke at cruck apex

c. Cruck truss adapted
for low-pitched roof

e. Crown post roof

f. King post roof

d. Two-bay box-framed structure

48. What sort of timber-frame?

49. Cruck-trussed barn at Halton, Runcorn, Cheshire
The raised cruck trusses have extended tie-beams, collars and a yoke detail at the apex. There are two post and beam trusses at the end of the barn.

Cruck construction

In cruck construction, pairs of stout, inclined timber members were spaced at intervals along the building to collect roof loads by means of ridge purlin, side purlins, and wall plates and transmitted them to the ground. Each cruck truss consisted of the two inclined cruck blades together with one or more horizontal members acting as tie-beam, collar or yoke according to position between floor and ridge. The blades, often sawn from a single tree-trunk to make a matching pair, might be straight or distinctly elbowed but usually were tapered and slightly curved from base to apex. The heavy purlins helped prevent the frame from collapsing sideways but in this they were assisted by straight or curved 'wind braces'. Cruck frames of this general description have been used for houses and farm buildings in the countryside (and sometimes in the towns) in most of Britain (except for a closely defined zone in the east and south-east) at least from medieval times until the late seventeenth century, and types of construction based on the cruck idea remained in use especially for farm buildings and certain minor industrial buildings until well into the nineteenth century.

The enclosing walls could be of any material. It seems likely that early cruck-framed buildings had walls of earth or turf; later, timber-framed walls were used, and these were replaced by stone or brick, though in some cases the new walls were simply planted on top of the old and an apparently solid gritstone wall may conceal a timber-framed wall itself cladding a set of cruck trusses.

50. House at Somersham, Suffolk
This house under demolition shows the main structure of posts and beams and the subsidiary structure of studs and rafters.

51. House at Benhall, Suffolk
In this house the structural timber-framing has been covered with a plaster cladding which in turn has the fanciful decoration moulded and painted called 'pargetting' which is characteristic of East Anglia.

Box-frame construction

In box-frame construction horizontal and vertical timber members were joined together to form the frame of a wall whose panels were infilled or covered with some cladding material. The vertical members might be structural posts or non-structural studs, the horizontal members were structural sill, wall plate or tie beam or were non-structural rails. Horizontal and vertical members were connected with specially designed joints to form a self-sustaining box, assisted by inclined members or braces to give some triangulation. The roofing was a separate item, the slate or tiles or thatch or any other roofing material being carried on separate pairs of rafters or by a combination of rafters and roof truss. These elements rarely revealed themselves on the outside of buildings, but, internally, the roof trusses, especially, demonstrate the skill and the architectural sensitivity of carpenters working on quite unpretentious buildings.

The timber members of the wall could be exposed or concealed. In so-called 'half-timbered' buildings the timber was exposed and the spaces in between, the panels, were filled with wattle and daub or, eventually, brick. Many such buildings, especially in South Lancashire, Cheshire, and the West Midlands

52. Bartholomey House, Lewes, Sussex
This house which appears to be built of brick is in fact timber-framed. The structural timber has been covered with 'mathematical tiles' specially shaped to imitate brickwork.

generally, as well as in Eastern Wales, made great play of the patterns of timber and panel, following the custom of blackening the timber and whitening the plaster panel to heighten the decorative effect. In other buildings both the timber and panel were concealed behind a cladding of plaster, plain tiles, weatherboard or those special tiles which we call 'mathematical tiles' because they were so regular, or 'brick tiles' because they imitated bricks.

There was a further type of construction related to the box-frame but used only on the more flimsy buildings. This is now called 'mud and stud', though local terms (such as 'clam staff and daub' in Lancashire) may be encountered. In this form of construction rough timber posts were set in the earth and joined together at the top to form a box while the wide spaces in between were filled by means of a sort of thin palisade of vertical staves liberally daubed with clay. It survived as a means of building various hovels until the late eighteenth century and it may be a very old-established technique indeed.

Stone, flint and cobble
Stone has always been wanted for the most prestigious buildings and good quality building stone was transported by water for considerable distances for such use. Where easily quarried or found as outcrop the material was also used for vernacular buildings of all types and it is fair to say that it is the predominant

though not usually the oldest, building material for vernacular buildings of all types in well over half of England and Wales, not to mention practically the whole of Scotland.

Even the merest glance will show that masonry walls differ considerably through the nature of the geological formation from which the stones were taken and from the method of laying the stones. (Quite apart from any architectural decoration which might have been introduced.) There are, however, some general practices which will be noticed. The most massive stones were used at the base of the wall; their weight discouraged use elsewhere and their size helped to distribute wall loads in the virtual absence of foundations as we understand them. The next largest stones were used as quoins or corner stones; if the stone generally available was of poor quality such as a soft chalk or a friable shale then superior stone was brought a few miles to make the quoins and other dressings even of vernacular buildings. Next the main part of the walls was raised up, according to one or other of the coursing techniques, with the larger stones at the bottom and smaller stones graduated up to the eaves; these walls were really formed out of two leaves of masonry, stones being laid to have flat sides to front and back with irregular ends tailing into the depth of the wall. Deep bonding stones were used at intervals to tie the leaves together and sometimes (as in carboniferous limestone sections of the Pennines) these bonding stones project to form a pattern of ledges on the wall.

Flints, cobbles and pebbles provided special problems. Flints are small and irregular, and even when broken or 'knapped' are difficult to use and were normally tied together by means of 'lacing courses' of brick or, sometimes, stone. Cobbles taken from river beds or morainic deposits are larger, but being rounded are hard to assemble in a wall except with very liberal use of clay or mortar as bedding. Pebbles taken from the sea shore make a delightful wall surface but

53. Lake District
The hard slate-like stones of the Lake District make very good masonry for vernacular construction. They were usually bedded in clay but the open joints at the surface help to give an attractive texture to the wall.

54. Dovecot and adjacent barn and foldyard at Minster Lovell, Oxfordshire
The walls show how versatile a material is the local Cotswold limestone.

again depend on plenty of mortar and backing or reinforcement of other material for their stability.

At certain times and in certain places walls of vernacular buildings were whitewashed or rendered with plaster or roughcast. Whitewash was used with carboniferous limestone, for instance, enhancing the pale grey of the stone and helping to protect the wide joints from leaching of the bedding material. Rendering with plaster and a smooth finish was popular in the early nineteenth century as an extension of the vogue for stucco in polite architecture.

Britain is blessed with an intricate pattern of solid geology and surface drift; areas of some uniformity, as in parts of North Wales, being more than balanced by other areas, as in Northamptonshire, where building stones seem to vary considerably within a few miles. Much of the attraction of vernacular architecture in Britain must stem from that variety.

Brick walling

While stone walling may cover the greatest area of vernacular buildings in this country, brick probably covers the greatest number—if only because of the vast spread of brick construction during the late eighteenth and nineteenth centuries. Although uniformity in the brick provides the basis for the economy of brickwork, the vernacular builders have shown that the results can be far from uniform.

Brick construction is relatively simple; the brick provides a material for general walling and for the formation of corners and openings; much of the mason's craft is exercised in the accurate reduction of the rude material into the desired shape, whereas the bricklayer's craft is exercised in the manipulation of standardised units. Traditionally, bricklayers have been able to avoid monotony in their brickwork through care in the selection of the size and colour of the bricks, through care in bonding (i.e. the way in which the bricks are laid together for strength and appearance), through the nature of the joints between bricks and through any patterning which is introduced into the brick surface.

At first bricks, from a great number of different brickmakers, were quite

55. House at Lacock, Wiltshire
Although it eventually became the cheapest walling material and was used in all parts of the country, brick was actually rather sparingly introduced into vernacular building construction, especially where stone was available. Here, in a stone-producing county, this house proudly displays Flemish Bond brickwork on its main elevation but retains stone for the dressings.

56. Cottage at Chilton Foliat, Wiltshire
Here the flint walls are held together with the aid of lacing courses of brickwork. The corners of the building and the door and window openings, which are difficult to make out of flint, are also built in brickwork.

irregular in size—and irregular in shape through poor control of the firing process, though still recognisable as bricks and generally of the proportions with which we are familiar. Gradually length and width became standardised though depth continued to vary from district to district and period to period almost to the present day. The colour of bricks used on vernacular buildings has never been standardised. Depending on brick earth and firing methods, neither precisely to be determined, colour varied from site to site, especially in the early days when bricks were made for each building and fired in clamps alongside the intended site. Jointing techniques were linked to the size and irregularity of the bricks: irregular bricks required deep bedding and a thick joint with plenty of mortar, regular bricks could have a thin joint, soft bricks used around windows could be rubbed till they needed only an almost invisible joint. Pattern came initially from the bonding, but bricklayers liked to take advantage of the variations in colour and texture resulting from the relative positions in the kiln of bricks when being fired, to produce patterns which, in vernacular buildings, would be started, abandoned, re-started and changed as the bricks came to hand.

Brick was the successor material to timber in the construction of vernacular buildings in most of the Midlands, and the Southern and Eastern Counties, and was used for many of the enormous numbers of cottages, farm buildings and minor industrial buildings erected during the Industrial Revolution.

Clay walling

Strange as it may seem there are thousands of buildings in Britain made of earth in the form of clay, cob, wychert (or wichert, a type of earth and chalk found in Buckinghamshire) and even turf which are still inhabited even though their walls are liable to return to the ground from whence they came unless carefully looked after.

The cob buildings of Devon are well enough known to observant holiday-makers and form the biggest concentration of earth-walled buildings in Britain, but Buckinghamshire, Leicestershire, Cumberland and Dumfries-shire are among the many other counties in which buildings made out of similar

57. House at Brightley, Devon
This substantial Small House is in fact built of earth but of the very durable mixture of clay and straw which as 'cob' is characteristic of the region.

89

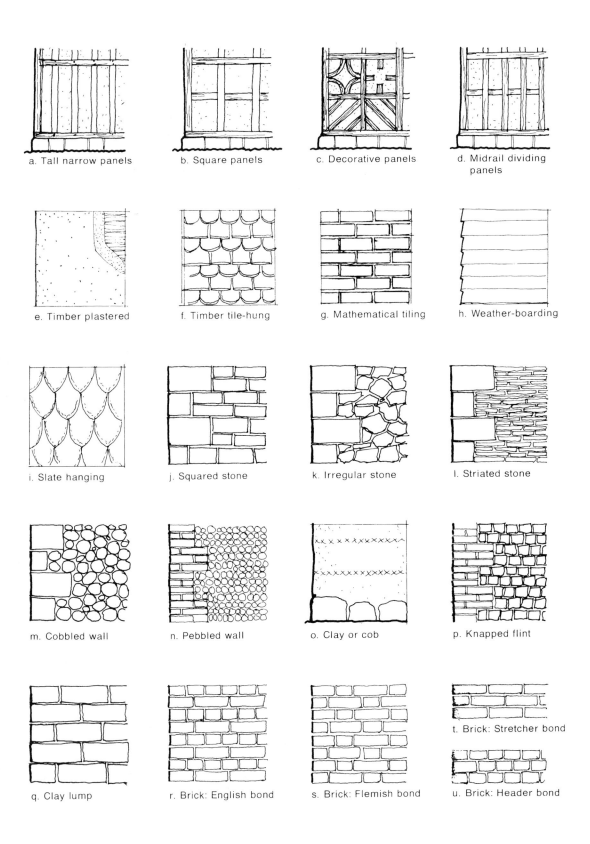

a. Tall narrow panels

b. Square panels

c. Decorative panels

d. Midrail dividing panels

e. Timber plastered

f. Timber tile-hung

g. Mathematical tiling

h. Weather-boarding

i. Slate hanging

j. Squared stone

k. Irregular stone

l. Striated stone

m. Cobbled wall

n. Pebbled wall

o. Clay or cob

p. Knapped flint

q. Clay lump

r. Brick: English bond

s. Brick: Flemish bond

t. Brick: Stretcher bond

u. Brick: Header bond

58. What sort of wall?

59. St. Andrew Street, Hertford
A selection of roof shapes: the house on the left has a gambrel roof, that on the right front is half-hipped with gabled wing, behind is an M-shaped roof having parallel gables with a valley between. All the roofs are covered in plain tile.

materials can be seen. Usually the earth or clay was dug near the site, trodden and mixed with straw and manure, raised on the wall, pared smooth with a hay-knife, allowed to dry and then levelled off for another layer to be placed. When the walls were finished they were rendered over with a stiff clay or lime plastering. As the clay of a well-constructed wall set really hard it could carry the loads of roof trusses and floor beams and there are two or even three-storey buildings made of this material whose rendered and colourwashed walls quite conceal their primitive origins.

The technique was very old-established, as recent excavations have shown, but many of the clay buildings are in fact fairly recent, being built in the late eighteenth century and early nineteenth century when there was a great demand for cheap construction and few really cheap materials.

Roof construction and roofing materials
So far we have only considered the roof of a building in association with its walls: in cruck-framed construction a roof was structurally part of the total frame; in box-framed construction and in all mass construction the roof was a separate structural item. However, we have also seen that one of the main tasks performed by the wall was the support of the roof and it is the interplay between the functions of a roof, the type of roof construction to be used and the nature of the roofing materials to be employed which gives rise to the variety of roofs gracing our vernacular buildings.

The function of a roof is obvious enough in that it is to keep the rain out of the building, but for many buildings this has to be done in a manner consistent with

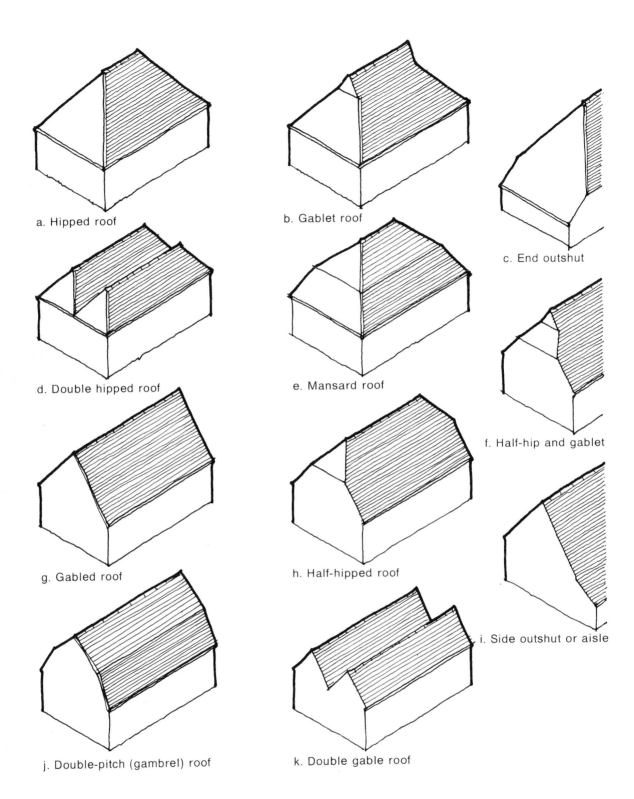

a. Hipped roof

b. Gablet roof

c. End outshut

d. Double hipped roof

e. Mansard roof

f. Half-hip and gablet

g. Gabled roof

h. Half-hipped roof

i. Side outshut or aisle

j. Double-pitch (gambrel) roof

k. Double gable roof

allowing the space within the roof to be used—for bedrooms, perhaps, in a house or cottage, for crop storage in a farm building, for storage of goods in a minor industrial building. These considerations have led to the use of two main types of roof: hipped (i.e. sloping all round) and gabled (i.e. coming to flat end walls) and the variations from these types such as the gambrel roof which has two roof slopes so as to give plenty of headroom, and the half-hipped roof with enough of a gable to allow a window to light the roof space, and which then finishes as a hip. The methods of roof construction vary principally between those which depend on sets of rafters jointed to provide their own stability and those in which the rafters transfer their loads to roof trusses; there are many variations, and those roofs which were meant to be seen from the inside developed very high architectural qualities, but generally the details of roof construction do not much affect the external appearance of buildings. Such a comment cannot be made about the nature of roofing materials, because the thatch and tiles, flags and slates sweeping down roofs to low eaves or piled in many dormers and valleys lend so much character to our vernacular buildings.

Generally the smaller the unit of roofing material the steeper the pitch or

60. What shape is the roof?

61. Roof trusses, Fiddleford Manor, Sturminster Newton, Dorset
The arch-braced collar beam trusses are cusped, as are the diagonal wind braces.

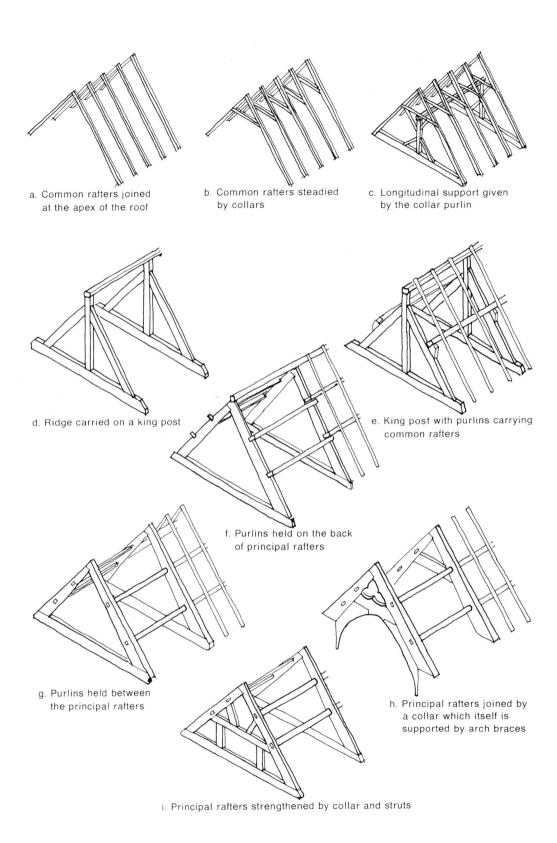

a. Common rafters joined
at the apex of the roof

b. Common rafters steadied
by collars

c. Longitudinal support given
by the collar purlin

d. Ridge carried on a king post

e. King post with purlins carrying
common rafters

f. Purlins held on the back
of principal rafters

g. Purlins held between
the principal rafters

h. Principal rafters joined by
a collar which itself is
supported by arch braces

i. Principal rafters strengthened by collar and struts

62. What sort of roof construction?

63. House at St. Nicholas, Glamorgan
The thatch on the roof of this house has been gently swept along so as to incorporate the dormer windows and avoid any sharp corners which might catch the wind or otherwise become vulnerable.

angle of sloping roof at which it must be laid. Again, the smaller the unit the greater the freedom in manoeuvring the roof about obstacles. Thatch, the oldest of roofing materials, being based on bundles of reeds or straw, requires a steep pitch but can be swept around angles with such facility as to make the roof almost alive, part of the ground from which the thatched buildings rise. Plain tiles require almost as steep a pitch and have something of the same facility: the tiled roofs of Kent and Sussex, for instance, accommodate the shifts and turns of the old timber-framed roofs which they cover so as to give the very undulations of the roof a life of their own. Pantiles have to be used with more caution. They are often seen on steeply pitched roofs, because they have replaced a former thatch covering, but they can be laid on shallow roofs, though only on those of simple shape, avoiding valleys and hips. Stone flags of the type found in the

64. House at Thaxted, Essex

This roof is covered with hand-made plain tiles. Each tile is curved slightly both in its length and its width and this, together with some slippage, gives the 'natural' texture to the roof which is so different from that of precise machine-made tiles. The half-hip is finished in 'bonnet' hip tiles.

65. Market House, Tetbury, Gloucestershire

Thin stone tiles cover this roof. The tiles are laid in diminishing courses, the larger tiles at the eaves and much smaller tiles at the ridge. As the tiles are fairly small—compared to the huge flagstones of the Pennines—it is possible to mitre them at the hip of the roof.

**66. Cottages at
Hawkshead, Lancashire
(now Cumbria)**
One is not surprised to see
Lake District slates on the
roof of these cottages but
slates have also been used
as a wall cladding. From
the position of the windows
near the wall surface the
slates are possibly a
cladding to a timber
frame.

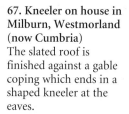

67. Kneeler on house in Milburn, Westmorland (now Cumbria)
The slated roof is finished against a gable coping which ends in a shaped kneeler at the eaves.

68. The Old Toll House, Copgrove, Yorkshire, W.R.
The steep pitch of the roof suggests that the house was originally thatched and the courses of flagstones which protected the top of the wall from dampness have been retained when the house, like so many in its neighbourhood, was re-roofed with pantiles.

Pennines are heavy at the eaves, though lighter near the ridge, and they also are best used over simple roofs on gabled buildings. The stone tiles of the Cotswolds are made of smaller pieces, so are used at greater slopes and cover magnificently the intricately dormered roofs of that district. Slates were generally introduced fairly late to vernacular buildings; the grey-green Lake District slates being an expensive covering for superior buildings in the eighteenth century and the blue-purple Welsh slates being a cheap covering, either new or replacement, for humble and utilitarian buildings in the nineteenth century. Pantiles are usually fairly late and are often replacements for thatch on buildings of timber, clay or stone walls.

It is one of the happy accidents of vernacular architecture that walling and roofing materials tend to stem from similar roots and so give a unity to the two parts of the building. With timber-frame and clay goes thatch, with brick goes tile, with stone go flags or stone tiles or slate. It is sad that this association can no longer be guaranteed among buildings more recently erected.

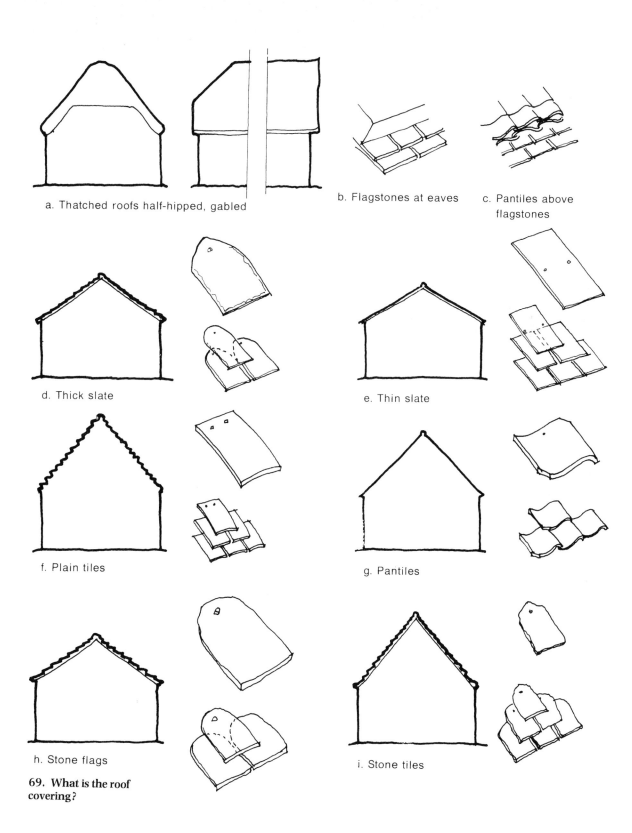

a. Thatched roofs half-hipped, gabled

b. Flagstones at eaves

c. Pantiles above flagstones

d. Thick slate

e. Thin slate

f. Plain tiles

g. Pantiles

h. Stone flags

i. Stone tiles

69. What is the roof covering?

Chapter 6

What architectural decoration may one find?

Looking at our simple vernacular buildings as works of architecture we can expect to find that in addition to well-proportioned shapes and agreeable materials there will be some appropriate architectural decoration. Scarcely any vernacular buildings are entirely without ornament, while those approaching the polite in architecture employ fairly sophisticated details in something like an academically correct manner. Most have more or less crude versions of what had once been up-to-date architectural decoration.

Confining our attention to the outsides of buildings we may glance at windows, doorways and chimney as parts of the building where decoration was apparently considered specially appropriate.

In the design of windows there are three items which particularly deserve attention: the overall shape, the mouldings and similar architectural details of the surround and the type of window frame. The overall shape responded partly to what was traditional or fashionable generally and partly to the shape of the room which was lit, and this in turn related to what was traditional or fashionable in room sections. Thus tall medieval rooms open to the roof called for tall windows like those of churches and these were decorated with tracery, arched and foliated heads and medieval mouldings. Low rooms of seventeenth century farmhouses called for long ranges of windows, each individual light being tall in proportion, but the whole range of lights, separated by mullions, being long in proportion. Rooms in the smaller houses of the eighteenth century might still be fairly low in ceiling height but square window shapes were popular. Then tall rooms and tall windows were reintroduced under Renaissance influence in the late seventeenth century Large Houses, later eighteenth century Small Houses and early nineteenth century Cottages, and the Georgian shape understood by all (except, perhaps, modern joinery manufacturers) was adopted. Mouldings changed from the splay of the medieval period through the square cut mullion, which survived surprisingly late, to the Renaissance mouldings of the Georgian period. The type of window frame related to window shape, materials available, function and, of course, tradition and fashion. Thus the earliest windows were unglazed and had internal hinged or sliding wooden shutters, then lattices of small glass panes were fixed directly to the mullioned windows or into wrought-iron hinged casements. The change to square and then upright windows marked the introduction first of side-hung wooden casements and then of sashes of even larger glass panes, sliding up and down in the tall windows and from side to side in the square windows.

Although the rest of a building might be seen from a distance, everyone who enters a building must make close acquaintance with the door and so the door and doorway provided a focus for ornament however sparse its extent. As in

70. House at Cerne Abbas, Dorset
Beneath the jettied upper storey of this building one may see the doorway with late medieval mouldings to the jambs and head and with quatrefoil carving above. The windows have moulded four-centred arched heads.

window design the shape, mouldings and fittings and the form of the door and its frame provided the basis for decoration. Medieval doorways were usually pointed, but there was a tendency for the arch to become flatter, and the four-centred arch which we associate with Tudor buildings percolated to the vernacular level in the sixteenth century. In the later seventeenth century square-headed doorways became more and more common, simple and unadorned in many timber and brick buildings, with decorated lintels in many stone walls. During the whole of the eighteenth century and much of the nineteenth century, vernacular buildings had simple square-headed doorways of much the same proportions as those used nowadays; the only major development was the use of fanlights, when the plan called for a lobby to be lit by a glazed panel, over the door and often under a semi-circular head. The Gothic doorways usually had several layers of mouldings under a drip or label mould originally intended to channel rain running down the wall and prevent it from blowing into the door. Mouldings of a less subtle, more geometrical kind were used during the transitional phase of the late seventeenth and early eighteenth centuries. Afterwards the Renaissance adornment and mouldings held sway, the simple square-headed doorway providing the starting point at first for bold, generous, florid surrounds with broken pediments and fat columns and later for

more restrained pediments, pilasters and architraves. The doors found with arched doorways were heavy planked and studded affairs hung on stout iron pins, opening inwards from a recess in the masonry itself and secured with a drawbar. For square-cut openings of the seventeenth and early eighteenth centuries rather lighter boarded doors were commonly used in heavy wooden frames and fitted with massive locks. With the Renaissance influence there came framed and panelled doors hinged in a light wooden casing and adorned with knob and knocker for the proud owner to polish. As the focus of attention in the elevation of a house, the doorway was sometimes more up-to-date in its design than the rest of the ornamental work. There is often a date worked into the lintel or the keystone—this is usually the date of erection or major alteration to the house but sometimes it represents an event, such as possession by a new owner or the wedding of an inheritor, and so the date should be accepted only if consistent with other items.

The flues emerging from open hearth or inglenook fires were at one time crudely accommodated in chimneys that were little more than fire-protected portions of a thatched roof. Once fireplaces became popular the chimney stacks rivalled windows and doors in their architectural adornment.

Chimneys of the sixteenth and seventeenth centuries of brick or, less often, of

72. Doorhead and plaque, Northgate, Heptonstall, Yorkshire, W.R.
Here the dour gritstone of the wall has been relieved by the dressed masonry of the doorway and the setting for the plaque above. Although the design is backward-looking, the double-curve of the mouldings has classical aspirations—as one would expect in the early eighteenth century. Again, the carving of the plaque which allows initials, date and figures to stand proud against a chiselled background is conservative, but the detailing suggests classical influence.

103

stone were usually very tall and very ornate. It was as if the householder, having introduced a fireplace into his draughty hall or built a new house with all the latest facilities wanted to share with his neighbours the feeling that this was no mere utilitarian matter of a new fireplace but was the beginning of a new way of life he was fortunate to be able to afford. In northern and western parts of the country quite simple chimney stacks served the fireplaces or inglenooks of the seventeenth century farmhouse; the stacks might be remarkably tall, chimney breasts might project massively from the gable walls but their architectural decoration was confined to simply moulded caps, perhaps incorporating a very discreetly hidden datestone.

The designers of the simple vernacular buildings employed some ingenuity in ringing the changes, period by period, on the limited range of architectural details which they allowed themselves to employ. The details would rarely stand up to scholarly examination, sometimes they were laughingly misused; at least one Rutland village is largely built out of mason's rejects from a nearby quarry. But their persistence in employing these details even in the face of quite intractable building materials reminds us of the care which they took in quite humble examples of vernacular architecture.

73. Window in Knutsford, Cheshire
The tall window shape matches the proportions of the rooms inside, the window head is formed in cut and rubbed bricks in the wall of brickwork, the sill is of stone, the better to drain away rainwater and the double-hung sash window with small panes relates well to the window shape.

74. What sort of architectural decoration?

GOTHIC –

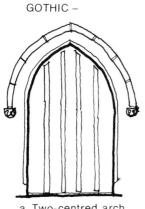

a. Two-centred arch doorway

b. Two-light window, foliated head

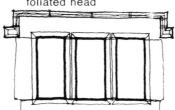

c. Three-light mullioned window

d. Chimney in stone

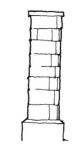

l. Cylindrical chimney stack

TRANSITIONAL –

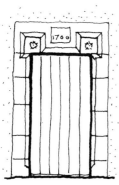

e. Decorated lintel to doorway

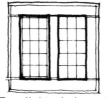

f. Two-light window with architrave surround

g. Square window with segmental arched head

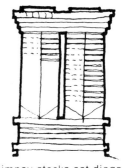

h. Chimney stacks set diagonally

RENAISSANCE –

i. Surround to doorway

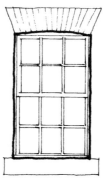

j. Tall window, double-hung sashes

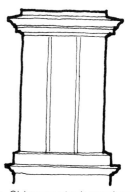

k. Chimney stack serving three flues

Chapter 7
What about the interior?

In looking at plans and cross-sections of houses we have already noted that basic requirements were a place for living (including cooking, eating and meeting people) and a place for retiring (including sleeping, seeking privacy and storing valuables) together with at least one source of heat for comfort and cooking. In Chapter 4 we saw how these activities generated the plans and cross-sections of domestic buildings and in subsequent chapters we have seen how, with the materials and constructional methods available, the vernacular builders clothed those activities in actual structures and how they made decorative what could have been merely utilitarian. Having seen the interaction of activity and construction on the outside appearance of the house we can now look at interiors and especially at the importance of the heat source in the design and character of the principal rooms of the house.

There are two factors which must be borne in mind. One is the importance of status in the design of interiors as well as exteriors of vernacular houses. The other is the difficulty in directing our minds to the way of life for which a contemporary interior was originally designed and therefore deciding upon the original appearance of an interior.

The broad divisions between Large House, Small House and Cottage have effects on interior as well as exterior design. A Large House with one to two cross-wings displayed for all to see the social status of its owner. It also reflected internally, in the number of rooms and the number and nature of the heat sources, in the differentiation between the open hall and the cross-passage, between the first-floor solar and the ground-floor cellar, and in the varying degrees of decoration applied to the structural members or the wall surface of each room, the relative status of one room against another. A Small House, say of baffle-entry plan, expressed the limited but significant position in society of the farming family which occupied it, but the access to the lobby and from the lobby to other rooms or to the upper floor expressed a delicate balance of relationships between different generations, between different members of the family and its resident servants. A single-fronted Cottage had no great status to express, but here again the difference between the parlour fireplace, the kitchen range and the scullery copper demonstrated variations of status even at a very humble level of society.

In contrast to the exterior where appearances may go through little change from original construction to the present day, the internal arrangements of a building are those which suit the present-day way of life rather than that originally intended. Indeed in our highly mobile society Great House, Large House, Small House and Cottage may represent stages in the life of a single family. The 'yuppy' couple park their Porsche and Mini outside a modernised Cottage, they start their family in an adapted Small House, teenage children ride ponies in the paddock of a Large House whose rooms are ideal for business entertaining. Family flown, the couple revert to a Small House or Cottage before entering the local Great House which has been converted to offer residential care. Each house may have been adapted and furnished for our contemporary way of life, but in looking at old houses we are most interested in that for which the building was originally designed. How can we find out?

The building itself can, of course, tell us a lot. The archaeological investigation of a house can best take place when building work is in progress, especially when that involves stripping away layers of earlier modifications. Thus work to the roof can indicate by smoke blackening the site of an original open hearth; modifications to rafters or ceiling beams can show how the hail fireplace was inserted in the sixteenth century; stripping the decayed Georgian or Victorian ceiling plaster may reveal the moulded joists of a former parlour ceiling; stripping layers of blocked-up fireplaces may reveal the original wide-arched hearth and its attendant spice cupboard and keeping holes. Of course the act of stripping away the evidence of history is not necessarily to be applauded, but where changes have to be made the opportunity for archaeological investigation is there.

Even when the building has been stripped as far as is desirable or feasible to its original condition the spaces and structure may not automatically specify hall or parlour, bedroom or granary. We then turn to documentary evidence. There may be contemporary descriptions available: Harrison in 1577 and Carew in 1602 tell us what was happening to the internal design of houses in different parts of the country in the late sixteenth and early seventeenth centuries. Celia Fiennes wrote quite clear descriptions of some of the houses and inns where she found accommodation on her travels in the late seventeenth century—her miserable experience at Aitchinson Bank in Scotland gives the reader an unforgettable impression of the 'Black House' type of dwelling and its unfamiliar peat fire.

Novelists such as Dickens, Hardy and Lawrence understood domestic arrangements and we can put ourselves into their house and cottage interiors just as readily as we can relate to the individuals and the family situations which are the subjects of the novels. The interiors of houses in Harlem and Amsterdam are familiar from popular Dutch paintings and the eighteenth- and nineteenth-century interiors in this country were quite faithfully depicted by local artists either as naive paintings or as part of a romantic fashion in the history of art. From the middle of the nineteenth century photographs abound to tell us about surviving interiors of earlier periods as well as, for instance, the way the machinery was fitted into an attic loomshop, or the slopstone in the scullery, or the tea caddy onto the mantlepiece of a worker's cottage.

Legal documents can sometimes illuminate the way of life enjoyed in a type of building or even a specific house. Sale particulars listing rooms and their uses may be available for Large Houses or Small Houses on estates sold during the nineteenth or early twentieth centuries; newspaper announcements advertising forthcoming auctions or sales by private treaty may be found to cover the same period. Wills do not often say anything about house interiors, but inventories of the goods and chattels of the deceased may be very informative, especially where room names are given along with the lists of items. The most useful inventories from this point of view are those of the late seventeenth and early eighteenth centuries and are most helpful, partly because this was a critical period in vernacular domestic design, and partly because they abound in the various county record offices, many having been transcribed into readable typescript. Where the neighbours who prepared the inventory and gave the valuations followed a logical route through the house one can imagine its layout, establish the room names and picture, through the various contents, the intended purposes of each room. Even if a specific inventory for a house under study cannot be identified, one related to a nearby or similar house can still be very useful.

Whether by the application of general information to an actual house or by the discovery of records relating to that house at a specific time one can find out about the way of life the building was meant to house and invest the dry archaeology with the indications of lively activity.

While we may be primarily interested in the original design of a house it is important to recognise the various stages in the development of an interior either because it represents events in the life of a particular family or because the stages represent developments in domestic design as a whole. For instance, a wing added to a yeoman's Small House may show that briefly the family had gained landowner status, the head of the household being eligible to serve as sheriff or even Parliamentary knight of the shire. The partitions inserted into a Large House, on the other hand, may represent the various stages in the decline of the building to farmhouse and then set of cottages. Generally, however, successive generations of houses reflect in their designs the increasing aspirations of their occupants. Thus there is a tendency for more living spaces to be arranged at more levels for more specified functions as each generation succeeded its predecessor. Greater prosperity called for greater comfort, more fixed and more moveable furniture and decoration increasing in quantity and sophistication. This applied at all social levels and can be seen in the labourer's cottage as well as in the farmhouse, and in the Rectory as well as in the Manor House.

The demand for more space meant that the basic suite of two zones* for living and sleeping in the medieval farmhouse had expanded to become the eight rooms of the early-nineteenth-century Double Pile Small House. The desire for a house on more than one level meant that such a house had four bedrooms above four living rooms, probably with a loft in the roof space and a cellar under some of the ground floor at least. The tendency towards greater specialisation meant that the living room shed some of its functions to kitchen, dairy and scullery while the parlour spawned bedrooms, pantry, granary and study. The desire for greater privacy was helped by the multiplication of rooms and also changes in communication, whereby staircases rose from halls or lobbies and into corridors rather than straight into rooms, while rooms themselves opened off halls or corridors rather than off each other. The provision of subsidiary staircases meant that resident servants had direct access to bedrooms from a mess room which might have its own external door, while elderly relatives could move between private parlour and individual bedroom without disturbing the rest of the household. The desire for more comfort meant that more rooms were capable of being heated so that the one hearth and one fireplace of a manorial hail might be succeeded by the dozen fireplaces and the 'Twelve Apos-

* Depending on the size and location of the house, these were simply two rooms or were amplified, e.g., with extra service rooms to expand the living zone or extra parlours and chambers to expand the sleeping zone.

tles' chimney stacks of a late-seventeenth-century Large House. Some of the heated rooms were made even more comfortable by panelled walls and plastered ceilings. More readily available window glass and better joinery techniques meant that double-hung sashes in tall windows gave more daylight and more easily controlled ventilation than the shuttered casements of heavily mullioned and transomed windows of a century earlier. The tokens of greater comfort often provided opportunities for more stylish display. Thus, not only were there fireplace and panelling in the parlour, but the fireplace surround, the over-mantel, the cornice and dado showed that the householder and his joiner and cabinet-maker were familiar with the pattern books of fashionable designers.

These indications of the rising standard of living enjoyed by all levels of society from the late medieval period to the late nineteenth century may be seen in the developing stages of house design. The interior reflected the improving way of life, the exterior made generally visible the architectural consequences of that improvement.

Attics, garrets and cellars

One aspect of the demand for more space and the increased specialisation of room function in houses lay in the development of space above and below the main living accommodation. We have seen already that the basic single-storey dwelling extended into loft space within the roof and over part or all of the main living accommodation; we have also noted that as the lofts became storeys there was further development into the roof space and below the ground floor. The layout and constructional implications of these interiors deserve a mention.

An area in a roof space is nowadays usually called the attic, but this is a term in classically-based architecture for a room above the cornice. One traditional word is indeed the loft, or its relative the cock-loft (and the Welsh croglofft); another word once used in Norfolk and Suffolk is the vance, but the most appropriate word in the context of vernacular architecture is the garret.

The garret may be entirely in the roof space as in the house at Benhall in Suffolk (51), within a double-pitch roof designed for the purpose as in the house at Lacock in Wiltshire (55), or partly in the roof space, but with low side walls. The garret space may be undivided or partitioned into several rooms. There may, of course, be separate garret spaces in separate wings.

The garret may be lit by windows in gable walls at each end of the roof space, by dormer windows ranging from the eyebrow dormers of a thatched roof to the carefully designed dormers in the true attic of a Georgian house in the Cotswolds, by rooflights within the slope usually of a slated roof, or by small windows near the head of a wall and down at the floor of the garret.

Construction varied with the traditions of the locality, but special arrangements were often made to provide headroom. One way was to make use of upper crucks, curved inclined principal rafters like true crucks, but rising from the beams at garret floor level; another was to introduce cranked feet to the principal rafters of more orthodox construction. Greater headroom was achieved where the tie beam of a truss was cut leaving stubs at each end braced back to a lower tie beam at garret floor level. For the gambrel (or double-sloped) roof special roof trusses were devised.

There is some evidence that originally garrets were loosely floor-boarded, but as their use became integrated into the design of the house permanent flooring and permanent access was provided. One type of floor—the plaster floor—became particularly associated with the garret. The plaster floor consisted of wooden beams and joists as in a normal timber floor, but with laths or reeds instead of floorboards across the joists, topped with several inches of a gypsum-based concrete and then finished with a smooth surface of gypsum plaster. There seem to have been three main reasons for use of this type of floor construction at garret level: to provide a smooth surface (and this was the reason given in an early documentary reference to plaster floors at Chatsworth in 1556); to produce a dry uniform surface without cracks or gaps; or to produce a fire-proof layer immediately underneath a fire-prone thatched roof. As one would expect, plaster floors are most often found in midland counties of England where gypsum is available, but lime-based versions were used elsewhere. These floors were not entirely confined to use in garrets as they may be found as the intermediate floors in two-storeyed cottages.

Garrets were used for storage, for sleeping, or for domestic industry. The main storage use, as found in the Costwolds for instance, was the storage of cheeses on racks where they could be turned regularly, but grain was also stored in arks, chests, or partitioned bins while fleeces of wool which had to be kept in secure and dry locations were also stored and here and there the machinery for raising the fleeces to garret-floor level survives in the building.

As one might expect, garrets are found early in urban vernacular buildings where the need to build high was most pressing, but they began to appear in numbers in the countryside from about 1660. Naturally, they are associated with the larger vernacular houses, but they can also be found in farm buildings such as granaries, and minor industrial buildings such as water mills and early textile mills.

It was easier to build upwards rather than excavate downwards and so garrets were more common than cellars. The term 'cellar' when found in early documents usually refers to a ground-floor storage room, but cellars partly or even entirely in the ground are associated with merchants' houses in the medieval period and are well represented in Southampton. In more ordinary houses cellars in the modern sense may be found on steeply-sloping sites, below the parlour when it was floored with joists and wooden floorboards, or below the whole house. Sometimes it appears that a cellar was excavated below an existing parlour when a new boarded floor was to be inserted. In the eighteenth century the main floor was usually carried over the cellar with beams and joists, but vaults of stone or brick were also found. For a short time cellar workshops were used at a half-level below cottages in the industrial areas.

Hearth and Fireplace

It is impossible to exaggerate the significance of the hearth in the design of vernacular houses in this country from their origin right up to modern times. Indeed, it has been suggested that the house began as a shelter for fire and that it was fire that made the house sacred. The practical importance of the fire as the provider of heat and light was reflected in the symbolic importance of the fire as distinguishing the house for humans from all the other 'houses' for industrial, agricultural or religious purposes. The hearth and its hearth-

75. Interior of Scotch Green Farm, Goosnargh, Lancashire
This room was most probably open to a roof supported by cruck trusses and with an inglenook and chimney hood beyond the tie-beam. The hood was replaced by a stone fireplace including a cast-iron kitchen range. The built-in cupboard and set of drawers alongside are a common feature in the region.

stone, the base for the fire, have corresponding practical and symbolic importance, establishing the position for the fire and the proof that fire was in fact intended to burn in a house.

The fire provided heat and light in the evening and in winter and provision for cooking at all times of the year. Fuel ranged from wood through furze, peat, dried turf and dung to coal (and, more recently oil, gas and electricity). Cooking devices included cauldron, pot, frying-pan and kettle on chain or crane over the fire, spit and Dutch, or heat-reflecting, oven in front of the fire and bakestone or griddle alongside the fire, with the bread-oven as a separate item or one incorporated with others in a cooking range. Developments in controlled combustion of the available fuel marched hand in hand with developments in cooking methods and changes in diet. All influenced the location and form of the heat source. Major changes in domestic design, especially the insertion of the intermediate floor in open hall-based houses have been associated with improvements in the design of hearth or fireplace.

Undoubtedly the earliest use of fire in vernacular dwellings was by way of the wood-burning fire on a hearthstone located at or near the centre of the floor in a hall open to the roof. This was true whether the hall was a substantial structure, with elaborate roof construction hidden in a gloom illuminated sparingly by the flickering flames, or whether the hall was a small low room with sparks flying up to touch a turf underthatch. Combustion of the wooden logs on the fire was helped by the use of a simple firedog, or later a pair of dogs or andirons, which also provided a rack for the spits on which meat was cooked. Smoke was directed upwards, to deposit soot on the roof timbers, while being absorbed by the thatch or encouraged out through vertical or horizontal louvres.

Control of the fire on the hearth was helped through the use of a fireback stone, wall, or reredos. Control of the smoke was helped by plastering the roof trusses above and to one side of the hearth, so that smoke was concentrated in a smoke-bay and could evacuate through a louvre or primitive chimney at the ridge. Such smoke-bays are characteristic of Small Houses in the south-eastern counties of England in the fifteenth and early sixteenth centuries. Protection from both smoke and downdraught was given by the dais canopy, a timber or plaster ceiling coved from a beam running over the edge of the dais down to the partition wall at the upper end of the hall. The internal jetty found in some timber-framed Small Houses may have helped to give similar benefit. Another way of controlling smoke in the smallest houses was by means of a smoke-hood of wickerwork plastered with clay and held over the hearth at a low level but rising to a wooden chimney at the ridge.

The central hearth remained in use in Large Houses long after its deficiencies must have been painfully apparent. At least in the larger halls it did provide a central source of heat and light able to serve all corners of the room. In small kitchen/living rooms a central position would have been very inconvenient and it is hardly surprising that the hearth migrated to a gable wall or some transverse wall or partition. In such smaller houses the hearth rarely moved to either of the side walls for low eaves made the formation of a chimney stack to control the smoke so much more difficult. Generally a timber, stone or brick wall behind the fire absorbed the reredos and allowed an ever more effective fire-hood to be produced either as a 'hanging lum', projecting in the Scottish fashion from the wall over the fire, or as part of an inglenook with a timber, stone or brick pyramidal hood drawing smoke from hearth to chimney stack.

The inglenook, found in many parts of the country but especially popular and long-lasting in the North of England, has sometimes been called a 'room within a room'. One side of the inglenook was the gable wall or a transverse partition wall in the house. Another side was the front wall of the house with the little 'fire window' illuminating the inglenook during daytime and indicating to visitors where the subject of the visit was to be found. The third side was a partition of about head height acting as the back to a fixed settle snugly

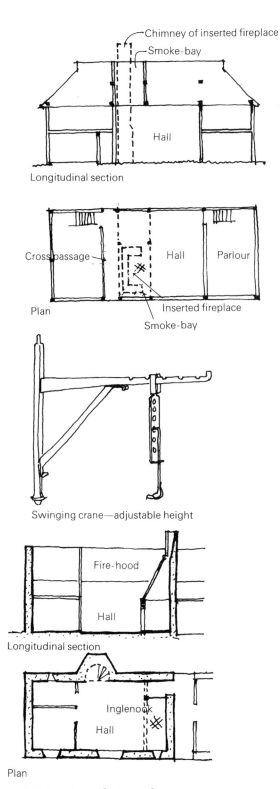

Chimney of inserted fireplace

Smoke-bay

Hall

Longitudinal section

Cross passage

Hall

Parlour

Plan

Inserted fireplace

Smoke-bay

Swinging crane—adjustable height

Fire-hood

Hall

Longitudinal section

Inglenook

Hall

Plan

76. Interiors: what sort of hearth and fireplace?

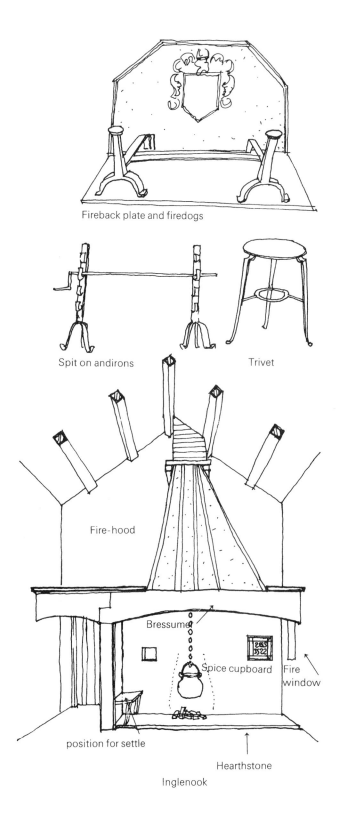

Fireback plate and firedogs

Spit on andirons

Trivet

Fire-hood

Bressumer

Spice cupboard

Fire window

position for settle

Hearthstone

Inglenook

113

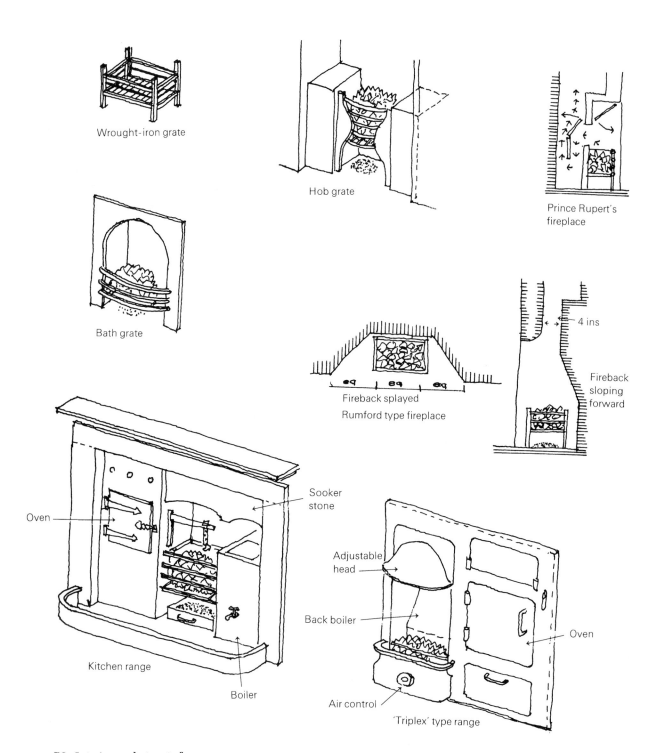

Wrought-iron grate

Hob grate

Prince Rupert's fireplace

Bath grate

Fireback splayed

Rumford type fireplace

4 ins

Fireback sloping forward

Oven

Sooker stone

Kitchen range

Boiler

Adjustable head

Back boiler

Oven

Air control

'Triplex' type range

76. Interiors: what sort of hearth and fireplace? (continued)

114

protected against draughts. The floor of the inglenook consisted of the extended hearthstone. The ceiling was largely provided by the fire-hood rising from the beam which defined the inglenook. The fire-hood contained hunks of meat and sides of bacon curing in the peat smoke while from a beam across the hood was suspended the iron chain which held cauldron and other cooking pots over the fire. Recesses in the wall acted as 'keeping holes' for the candles or, with a wooden cupboard door, as the 'spice cupboard' where salt and spices could be kept safe and dry. The hearth itself was made up of flagstone or slate, or of small stones pitched end-up in a pattern, or of bricks and tiles, depending on the locality. Sometimes the wall behind the fire was protected by a cast-iron fireback, as was commonly done in fireplaces where the foundries of the Weald of Kent and Sussex found market. Andirons, fire irons, bellows etc., completed the furnishings of the inglenook.

Such a well-developed space remained in use even after an intermediate floor increased the usable capacity of the house and improved the comfort of the whole of the kitchen/living room. The inglenook arrangement was particularly suitable for peat fires, where subsidiary fires could be established when needed on the hearth, and was only finally abandoned with the development of coal-burning grates and the introduction of the kitchen range in the late eighteenth century.

The fireplace had been known at least from Norman times, and in major buildings had been introduced as the heat source in upper halls and solars at the same time as the central hearth was used in the open ground floor hall. At the vernacular level the fireplace came into use both to serve prestigious inner rooms, such as the parlour, and also the main living room in many parts of the country. The essentials of the fireplace were the fireback wall, the jambs, and the arch or beam, making a three-sided incombustible box, together with the hearth and a chimney rising to the brick, stone or timber chimney stack. Although some fireplaces were very wide and fairly deep they rarely gave the feeling of a room within a room, nor had the capacity of an inglenook.

Although any fuel could be burnt in a fireplace the design eventually proved the most satisfactory one for the burning of coal. Once called 'sea-cole' to distinguish it from charcoal and indicate the manner of its transport to London, bituminous coal, in fact, used to outcrop in many parts of Britain, and, from the seventeenth century onwards, filled the gap in the diminishing supplies of other fuel. It was the use of coal as much as anything that made possible the multiplicity of fireplaces in houses of the eighteenth and nineteenth centuries.

For effective combustion lumps of coal have to be packed together with provision of a draught from below. At the same time a place for the collection of ash below the fire is needed and also a means of drawing the combustion air through the coal while evacuating the dirty products of combustion out of the house. The result was the use of a wrought-iron basket, on legs, set in a fireplace. Variations included the use of stone or cast-iron hobs on each side of the basket grate to help contain the fuel and direct most of the draught to the underside of the grate; the platforms on the tops of the hobs were convenient resting places for kettles and pans. Another variation was the provision of an arched plate of iron or stone in front of the grate. This certainly improved the draught through the fire and up the chimney, but the merrily burning fire of this, the Bath grate, used up the coal too extravagantly for many households. The search for efficiency and economy led to the use of firebricks lining tapered sides and an inclined back to the fireplaces directing the radiant heat of the fire into the room. However, the most effective device was the throat restrictor where smoke from the fire was drawn up through a slot restricted to 8 inches by 4 inches into the flue and so into the chimney stack. These improvements to the fireplace, where heating a room was the principal concern, lasted until the coal-burning fireplace passed out of general use in the middle of the present century.

Effective use of the coal fire, for cooking and water-heating as well as space-heating, came through the development of the cast-iron range characteristic of vernacular kitchen/living rooms from the late eighteenth century to the early twentieth century. In a way the range was a development of both the hob grate and the Bath grate, except that hobs were replaced by oven water heaters, and the arched plate became what in Yorkshire was called the 'sooker stone'. Although at first the oven was heated by a separate fire and the boiler simply by waste heat from the side of the grate, the fully developed range incorporated a series of flues and dampers whereby hot air from the coal fire could be directed round oven and boiler or hot plate as required. Indeed the range became a remarkably versatile piece of dometic equipment. As well as space- and water-heating the range provided for baking, boiling, stewing, frying and plate-warming simultaneously or separately; the mantlepiece provided a shelf for items of decoration or utility, the racks in front of the fire or above the range provided for clothes-drying; the deep ash pit accumulated cinders or ash for various purposes while the gleaming fender served to corral chicks and pet lambs in season. The successors to the range were the smaller, neater and more efficient 'Triplex' range of the early twentieth century, and heat-storage cookers of the 'Aga' type, cleaner and more economical, but lacking the romance of the old black-leaded range.

The main hearth or fireplace in the vernacular house was used for whatever was the staple food of the locality: porridge, stew, oat-cakes, etc., cooked in pan, cauldron, bakestone or griddle, but eventually all families expected to be able to eat wheaten bread baked in an oven. Residual heat was commonly the basis for baking, whereby a dome-shaped chamber, formed of stone or brick or a fixed fireclay lining, was heated by twigs, which were then raked out, and the bread baked in the heat remaining in what was a heavily insulated oven. The door to the oven was usually a loose piece of stone or slate sealed with dough, but tight-fitting cast-iron doors eventually became available. Most domestic ovens were placed alongside or within the fireplace, but sometimes they were set in a roofed projection from the chimney breast. Such ovens remained longest in use in those parts of the country without coal supplies, but eventually, as coal became universally available, they were superseded by the ovens which formed part of the ubiquitous range.

From the common origin of firewood burning on a hearthstone the development of the hearth and fireplace has varied appreciably from one country to another: the Continental stove with its massive tiled exterior and the American metal stove with its snaking flue are both foreign to our ideas on the principal domestic heat source. Within the British Isles the developments in Ireland, Scotland, Wales, Highland and Lowland England have all differed in detail and sometimes quite fundamentally. In all localities study of the heat source will contribute materially to the understanding of the vernacular interior.

Partitions, panelling and fixed furniture

Although the size and proportions of the vernacular interior may have been determined by use and construction the very means of defining space by walls, ceiling and floor gave the humble designer the opportunity of decorating the utilitarian.

The partition between hall and parlour was an instance of such an opportunity. The use of alternate thick and thin timbers in the 'muntin and plank' arrangement gave a rhythm to the design which was heightened by chamfers and other mouldings. Since the partition was located at the socially 'upper' end of even a tiny hall the decoration was appropriate as was the incorporation of a fixed bench in the partition. Seat and bench-ends may later have been removed, but mortices and peg-holes together with change of mouldings may guide the careful observer to their former location. Timber-framed partitions may also be decorative or provide the basis for painted decoration.

In larger and later vernacular houses the principal room was sometimes panelled as a sign of status and as a means of improving comfort. The development of joinery techniques is a subject in itself, but authentic panelling in vernacular buildings deserves close observation and study. On the other hand, the practice of moving panelling no longer fashionable for re-use in a humbler dwelling, as well as the occasional fashion for making vernacular buildings seem ever more authentic suggest that one must be cautious in accepting all panelling as original.

Ceilings, too, gave an opportunity for decoration appropriate to the use of the room. The decorative moulding of the structural members of the medieval roof trusses related to the design of the open hall and contrasts with the rough finish of trusses intended to be hidden behind plaster ceilings. Intermediate floor and ceiling construction led to quite elaborate moulding of beams and joists and the form of such mouldings and their stops is developing into another specialist study. From the sixteenth century onwards plaster ceilings became more fashionable than timber and the decorative patterns, though often crude in design and rustic in execution, followed, at an interval, the national trends. The limited life of such plasterwork, however, has meant that some work originally of some quality has been compromised by later maintenance and restoration.

Floors, again, varied in their design and construction according to the use and status of the rooms they served. Beaten earth was commonly accepted for living rooms though a timber floor was sought for the parlour. The need to establish or renew earthen floors led to folk practices such as inviting neighbours for a dance to harden the floor while making a frolic out of necessity. Where available, flagstones or slate paving stones were, of course utilised, but elsewhere, small stones gathered from the fields or river beds were pitched in patterns. Near the seaports imported paving bricks or 'pamments' came early into use and their manufacture developed to some extent in this country. Again, tiles, though expensive, were sometimes to be found in vernacular buildings.

One of the principal items of built-in furniture was the box bed. Surviving examples are practically confined to Scotland and Northern Ireland, with a few in Wales, but it seems likely their use was more widespread and Cumbria and the Pennines, for instance, give evidence for such a tradition. Another item of fixed furniture is the spice cupboard door. In spite of the enthusiasm of antique collectors in the past, many examples of quite elaborately carved spice cupboard doors survive in the Lake District. The bread cupboard of the same part of the

77. Built-in furniture: bread cupboard, The Common, Windermere, Westmorland
Dated 1715, this substantial cupboard was designed to be built into the partition between hall and parlour in a yeoman's farmhouse.

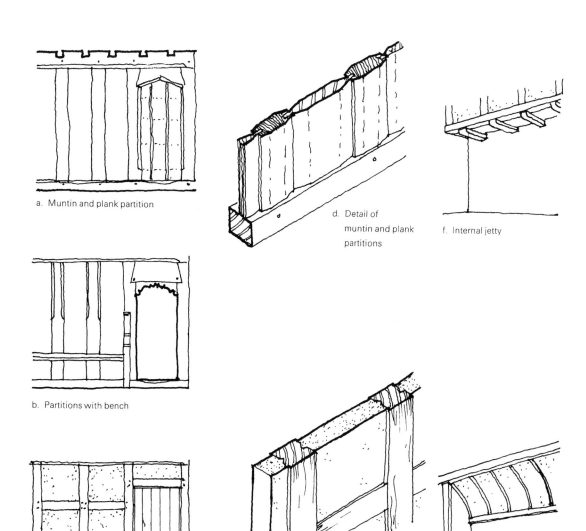

a. Muntin and plank partition

b. Partitions with bench

c. Timber-framed partition

d. Detail of
muntin and plank
partitions

e. Detail of
timber-framed partition

f. Internal jetty

g. Cove at dais end of hall

**78. Interiors: what sort of
panelling, partitions or
built-in furniture?**

country and the dresser of Wales are other items of fixed or built-in furniture. In both cases the use was there, but decorative joinery shows how the symbolic value was as great as the utility.

Wall paintings and plasterwork

In our concentration on planning and construction we sometimes forget that it is in the detailed treatment of interior wall, ceiling and floor surfaces that the occupier of a vernacular dwelling expressed his (or more likely her) decorative wishes and turned a house into a home. We know little about the surface treatment of early houses at the vernacular level. Floors seem to have been of beaten earth with patches of flat stone or pitched cobbles; walls seem to have been of the material itself in timber-framed buildings and roughly rendered with whatever was available in stone-walled buildings; ceilings were non-existent where the rooms of a single-storey building were left open to the roof. As long as the smoke from an open hearth burning wood or peat was allowed to rise unconfined there was little incentive to decorate the structural surfaces. Even the patterned straw underthatch known from South Wales may be a later improvement. It is by extensive smoke-blackening that we learn so much about the internal organisation of the medieval or sixteenth-century house.

With the revolution of the mid-sixteenth century onwards the situation changed and the opportunities multiplied. This was the revolution already mentioned whereby an intermediate floor was inserted in the open hall, the fire was confined to an inglenook or a fireplace, and a new great chamber was created in the upper part of what had been the hall. This revolution occurred in the design of new houses in the period as well as in the transformation of existing houses. From the mid-sixteenth century, therefore, at least in the more prosperous parts of England, wall paintings seem to have been introduced. Undoubtedly most of what had existed was lost in later alterations and renewals; few things about the house are quite so subject to fashion as wall decoration; but some paintings were covered in such a way that recent refurbishment has revealed them and we are gaining some idea of their nature. Generally the paintings were applied directly to timber-framed surfaces without acknowledgement of the pattern formed by timber frame and panel, or muntin and plank partition—for these were presumably the creatures of former fashion—otherwise they were painted directly onto plastered surfaces. The patterns, scenes and colours related to half-understood versions of fashionable scenes, to local or family activities or as overall patterns. The colours, insofar as they have survived, obviously depended on locally available pigments. In addition there were stained 'hangings', painted cloths as a crude version of tapestry, used occasionally earlier than and into the eighteenth century. Wallpaper was a luxury in Britain until the mid-nineteenth century. Throughout the period from the late sixteenth to the mid-nineteenth century plain limewash was used as a regularly renewed wall finish for its cleanliness, its light-reflecting and its disinfectant properties.

Ceiling finishes began as the counterpart to the floor construction which created the ceilings to ground-floor rooms. Heavily moulded beams and chamfered floor joists, even patterns of beams and joists, emphasised the decorative qualities of the newly comfortable rooms, especially the parlour. However, it was in plaster finishes that the newly-available decorative possibilities were best recognised and it was in the ground floor parlour and the first-floor great chamber that the plasterer was allowed greatest freedom in design and execution. The inspiration for the plasterwork originated in the late-medieval period and its designs, but it was probably the influence of some Great Houses, especially the royal palace of Nonsuch of 1540, and the rapidly spreading classically-based designs originating in Italy, but arriving by way of France and the Low Countries, which hastened the use of decorative plasterwork in vernacular houses. Designs developed from the heavily-ribbed early examples through the deeply-modelled late-seventeenth- and early eighteenth-century patterns to the more delicate designs of the late eighteenth and early nineteenth centuries. Many examples of plasterwork survive though understandably the designs have been distorted by generations of repair and restoration.

Wall finishes included wooden wainscotting, but also plasterwork especially around the fireplace. The overmantel designs were often quite elaborate, including armorial bearings to indicate the achievements or aspirations of what were often quite lowly families.

Plastered wall and ceiling finishes reduced draughts, helped to conserve heat and increased the comfort of houses from the mid-sixteenth century onwards, but coupled with documentary sources they tell us a lot about the quality of life enjoyed at various periods by different classes of people and sometimes by individual families.

Staircases

The means of access from one floor of a vernacular house to another is of interest in its position, its form and construction and its decoration.

One position commonly used was beside a fireplace, especially in a gable wall, the steps curving compactly round to fit in with the taper of the flue. Another was between front door and fireplace jambs in the baffle-entry plan, the staircase neatly turning round itself between ground and first floors. The rear wall position meant that a staircase could be accommodated in a shallow projection, or in a deeper rear wing to rise from one corner of the hall or kitchen/living room to reach the rooms above. Straight flight staircases could be located in many positions but were often used longitudinally or transversely in single-fronted Cottage plans. Early staircases were usually cramped and hidden; later staircases were more generous and prominently located.

The simple ladder survived to serve the small rural cottage in Wales until the nineteenth century, giving access to the 'croglofft' over the tiny parlour while its improved version as a companion-way set inside a cupboard was used more widely in one-roomed cottages. Variations of the spiral or winding staircase were made of separate stone steps fixed into the wall, as in a castle, or of solid baulks of timber around a central mast. A short-lived development in late-sixteenth-century Large Houses was the staircase with short flights rising from landing to landing round a solid central core. This was briefly developed into the 'cage staircase' where the solid core was replaced by four tall posts running the full height of the staircase; the risers and treads of the wooden staircase were framed into stringers which in turn framed into the posts. Finally, it was realised that the posts could be safely cut into separate newels and the

79. Staircase at Ashley, Cheshire
Two flights and a quarter-space landing are visible together with flat balusters and a square newel post cut to baluster shape.

versatile and long-lasting framed wooden newel staircase was the result. The dog-leg staircase, with two flights returned around a single newel, was a simpler version.

Opportunities for decorating the early ladders or winding staircases were limited but framed wooden staircases were prominently located and often quite ornate. The newel posts themselves were carved and the balusters were turned in a profusion of patterns. Vernacular joiners used the flat baluster as a simpler and cheaper version in staircases to attics or cellars of Large Houses, or more generally in Small Houses.

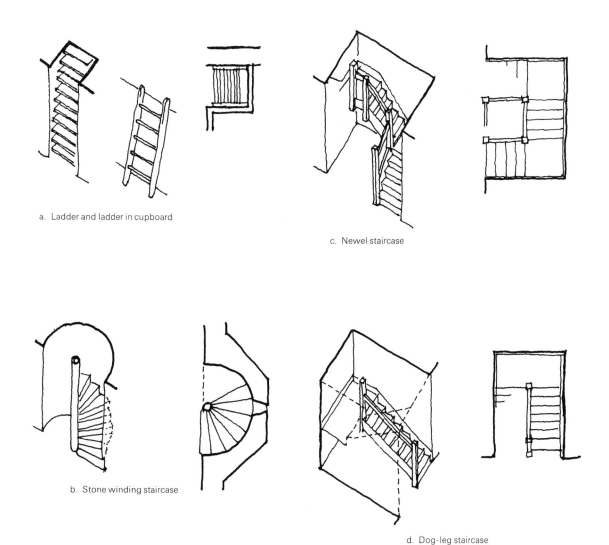

a. Ladder and ladder in cupboard

c. Newel staircase

b. Stone winding staircase

d. Dog-leg staircase

80. Interiors: what sort of staircase?

Chapter 8
How did the buildings develop?
How can we arrive at a date?

For many readers the procedure of unravelling the history of a building is a fascinating one but for complete fulfilment it has to lead to dates for the construction of the various parts, and especially of the oldest. The procedure has something of the fascination of a detective story: clues are assembled, false trails are trodden, but ultimately the mystery must be solved. In a detective story the clues placed in correct order lead to the murderer with an inevitability which real life detectives must envy. The interpretation of vernacular buildings is more like true criminal investigation than detective story writing: clues may lead towards a conclusion but rarely give a precise date. Indeed, just as the suspect's confession is usually one of the red herrings in the story so the actual date *on* the building may not, as we have seen, necessarily represent the date *of* the building.

There are two main sources of information which help to date buildings: documentary and architectural—the building itself and documents about the building or analogous to the building type. We are here concerned with what the building can tell us from external observation, for although its message may be far from clear it does relate to the specific building; very rarely can documentary information be tied to a specific vernacular building in the way that building accounts, for instance, can document a cathedral or palace. Observation and recording of a specific vernacular building can lead to a list of its characteristics: plan and section, use of materials, presence of decorative details. These can then be related to securely dated examples of comparable buildings. We can reasonably accept that a farmhouse which shares many or most characteristics with a dated farmhouse of similar size in the same district will also share its date. But a difference in status or location might mean a big difference in date. Since only a limited number of features, let alone complete vernacular buildings can be considered as securely dated, it is important not to rely on a single dating criterion. We should attempt to obtain approximate dates from as many features as possible, letting one item support or modify the conclusions drawn from another until a date within a fairly narrow band can be hazarded.

It may seem that decorative features would give quite close dating in the way that the mouldings of a pier in a church or the details around the portico of a great country house enable the experts to trot out a date practically to the year. But, as has already been hinted, there are special corrections which must be applied in the comparison of details from vernacular buildings. In the first place the date at which a feature is used will vary with the status of the building. Thus a particular type of window will be introduced at the Large House level (having been copied from some Great House), then come into use successively in Small Houses and Cottages and then, if appropriate, may be used on farm buildings or

81. Some aids to dating

124

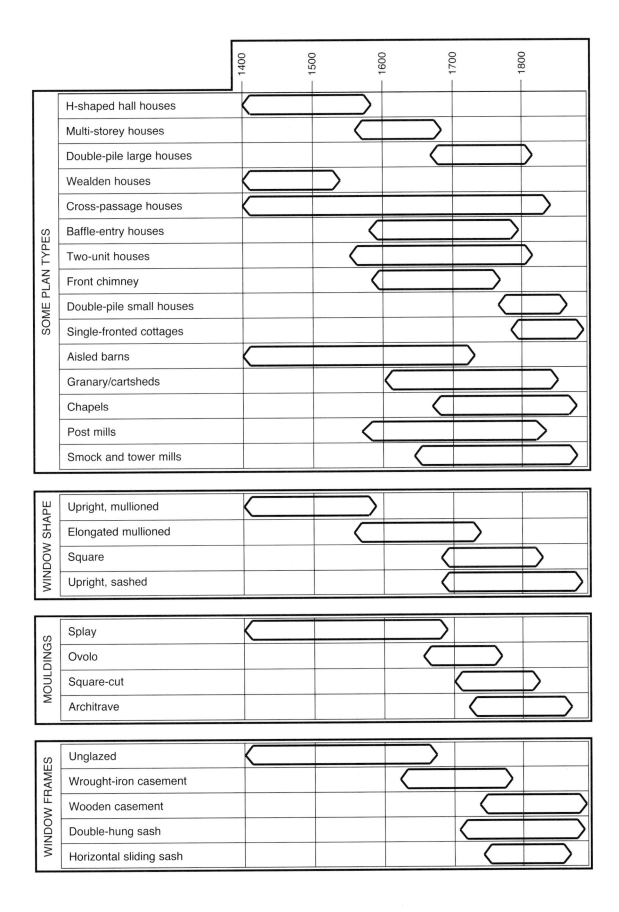

82. House in Town Street, Thaxted, Essex
This house shows work of two distinct periods: the narrow depth, low storey height and completely jettied upper floor indicate sixteenth or early seventeenth century work; the tall windows with double-hung sashes and the delicate cornice suggest late eighteenth century changes, though the bay windows indicate a possible early nineteenth century date. Although there are two main phases internal examination might reveal others.

minor industrial buildings. Secondly, the date at which a feature is used at a given level of vernacular buildings will fall within a period between the introduction of the feature and its abandonment at that level: some features were used for years by the more conservative builders, long after they had been abandoned by more inventive neighbours of the same social level. There were long periods of overlap in which traditional and fashionable details were in use simultaneously. Thirdly, the date will vary, as we have seen, according to the position occupied on the building: a house may have archaic mullioned windows, with splayed mouldings at basement level on the front and over the whole of the rear elevation, but have completely up-to-date sash windows, in classically moulded architrave surrounds, to light the rooms at the front. Fourthly, the date of a feature will tend to vary with the backwardness or otherwise of the district in which it was found—and even that is not consistent in time. Broadly speaking, features were introduced in the South-East of England and then adopted, with a time lag, region by region until they reached the northern and western extremities of Britain. Remote parts of North and West Wales and much of Northern and Western Scotland adopted practices long after

83. House in Weobley, Herefordshire

This late medieval building retains the exposed half-timbering on the upper floor but on the ground floor a stone wall has been built to meet the face of the jettied upper floor. Tall sash windows have been included in this ground floor masonry and the original windows at the upper level have been replaced by sash windows to match. Although the original steep pitch of the roof has been maintained modern tiles replace what was probably a thatched roof.

they had been abandoned in their places of origin. This generalisation is subject to modification in that formerly advanced parts of the country, such as East Anglia, subsequently became rather backward and in that there was some leap-frogging over districts, as trade routes or the accidents of location of influential works of architecture spread innovation into some rather unlikely districts.

One must also remember that few vernacular buildings survive unaltered and one may need to date successive phases which are all represented. The plan, for instance, may be that of a medieval H-shaped hall, the cross-section may be that of a late sixteenth century multi-storey house, the rear elevations may be the remnants of a seventeenth century modernisation whereas the front elevation has an eighteenth century applied façade in a different building material. All these are phases in the life of the building and all are significant. Some observers may be interested in the charm and relative correctness of the façade, others in the survival of evidence of the modernisation, still others will be principally interested in evidence of the earliest possible date of construction. All these interests are equally legitimate. Vernacular buildings provide opportunities for very wide ranging studies indeed.

Many buildings, of course, bear a date. This may not necessarily be the date

of construction; it may commemorate a marriage or it may indicate a change of ownership; but usually such a date signifies that some work was done to the building. The most likely place to find a date is on the lintel of the front door. Another common position is in a plaque over the door, though, again, we must beware of plaques moved from a different position or another property, or of modern plaques repeating a date for which the evidence may or may not be convincing. A less common position is on the outside of a chimney breast or on a chimney stack, both positions, no doubt, relating to the great social importance at various times of improvements to the heating system. Internally a date may appear on a fireplace surround—another token of heating improvements. Fixed pieces of furniture such as a spice cupboard built in a wall or a bread cupboard built in a partition often bear dates, though, again, one must be cautious about items brought from elsewhere to be fixed in quite convincing positions. Plasterwork also may include initials and a date in the decorative scheme. There were periods of popularity in the use of datestones. Harrison and Hutton, for instance, have shown that in the Settle area of Yorkshire dated lintels are most numerous for the period 1660–69 whereas in the Halifax area they peak in the perid 1630–39; but these peaks do coincide with periods of great interest in domestic vernacular architecture.

During the past 20 or 30 years there has been great success in the application of science to dating in archaeology and some of the techniques have proved helpful in dating vernacular buildings. Radiocarbon dating, which depends on measurement of the decay in radioactivity in organic matter, has not proved as useful as once expected for the period in which most vernacular buildings

84. Chimney stack, Lacock, Wiltshire
The symbolic significance of the hearth, fireplace and chimney stack is indicated by the careful way in which this is dated 1778. The chimney pots, as usual, are more recent.

85. St Mary's Street, Stamford, Lincolnshire
A detailed RCHM *Inventory* for Stamford gives histories and approximate dates for these buildings. From right to left there is a deep-plan house of probably 1748, a brick-walled and stone-fronted building of 1827 with its Gothic touches, and a house re-fronted in the mid-eighteenth century and heightened at the turn of that century. The former Eagle and Child inn, basically late medieval, has a coachway beneath plastered jettied gable.

were erected though still very useful in dating the evidence for their predecessors. Dendrochronology (or tree-ring dating) has proved more effective than was once expected. Scientists have established standard 'curves' or sets of widths for tree-rings against which samples of timber can be checked. Where sample and curve coincide and where appropriate corrections can be made, then a felling date for the timber can be accurately established. Although the growth of trees depends on many environmental factors, reliable dating sequences have been determined. The use of timber shortly after felling means that felling date and construction date are closely related. There was a good deal of re-use of timber in the past and the practice still continues, but the dating of re-used timber may further help in the study of the predecessors to our surviving vernacular buildings.

In attempting to assign dates to a vernacular building it is probably best to try

86. Cottages at Bossington, Somerset
At first glance these appear to be vernacular buildings incorporating a few architectural details found in the locality. But they are in the Vernacular Revival style as neither the organisation of the plan nor the full collection of details have that air of 'inevitability' which marks the continuous vernacular tradition. See Chapter 11.

to gain an overall impression of the building and, particularly, to decide into which broad plan-type it seems most naturally to fall, while bearing in mind that the cross-section, the vertical dimension, must be brought into play as well as the horizontal of the plan. Then one should look at the constructional system and the materials used: is it consistent with the plan-type for its region? Do the materials represent a re-casing of an earlier structure? Next one should look at the shape, mouldings and joinery of doors and windows, the size and details of chimneys and dormers, fancy gables and lead rain waterheads and other details, often less obtrusive, part functional and part decorative. All these can be compared with other, dated, examples which have been recorded in the neighbourhood or have been published in the books and journals. One can then establish a range of dates for the various features and a smaller range of dates which are common to all of them. This gives an approximate date for the building and one which can be substantiated—at least until some other piece of evidence comes to hand.

Chapter 9

What are the common regional variations?

The succeeding pages illustrate some of the common building types or details which are particularly well represented in the various regions of Britain. Very few of the features are exclusive to a single region: most are represented in adjacent regions or in the country as a whole. Some plan-types are found in all parts of the country but are expressed differently because of the different building materials which have been used. Some regions, quite small in themselves, include a diversity of building types and provide many building materials. The picture of vernacular architecture in some regions is clearer than in others because of the varying intensity of research which has been undertaken. Nevertheless the existence of regional variations has long been recognised and we are rapidly moving towards the time when the regional variations can be precisely defined, when definitive maps to show the distribution of characteristics on a regional basis can be confidently expected and authoritatively prepared.

Botanists are able to draw maps of the distribution of plants in this country; ornithologists are able to predict where types of birds may be seen nesting or passing over. The enthusiasts for vernacular architecture will soon have perfected their classifications and established their regional and local distributions. Their work will not thereby have ended any more than has the work of botanists and ornithologists. Just as plants may be found where they are not expected or birds make themselves homes in quite unanticipated locations so we will expect to find oddities: cross-passage houses in North Wales, crucks in Suffolk, mathematical tiles in Durham. Having established that certain features occur normally in certain places we shall be fascinated to speculate on why they occur abnormally elsewhere.

In the following pages there may be found a photograph of one building which seems to be typical of the region and a page of sketches of buildings or features which seem to make up regional character. Travels around the country will allow the keen reader to check off the various examples as they are seen and so add to his collection.

87a. Barn, with a horse-engine house attached, on a farm near Minehead, Somerset
Within the horse-engine house horses would have trodden a circular path rotating an overhead wheel which eventually, with the aid of various gears, powered a threshing machine or other machinery in the barn. This type of building, and especially its apsidal plan, is common in the West Country and is usually found with walls of local stone and quite often, as here, with roofs of thatch.

87b. Barn with horse-engine house attached at Temple Sowerby, Westmorland
The function and general shape are similar to the West Country example but the red sandstone walls and Lake District slate roof betray the north-western location of this building.

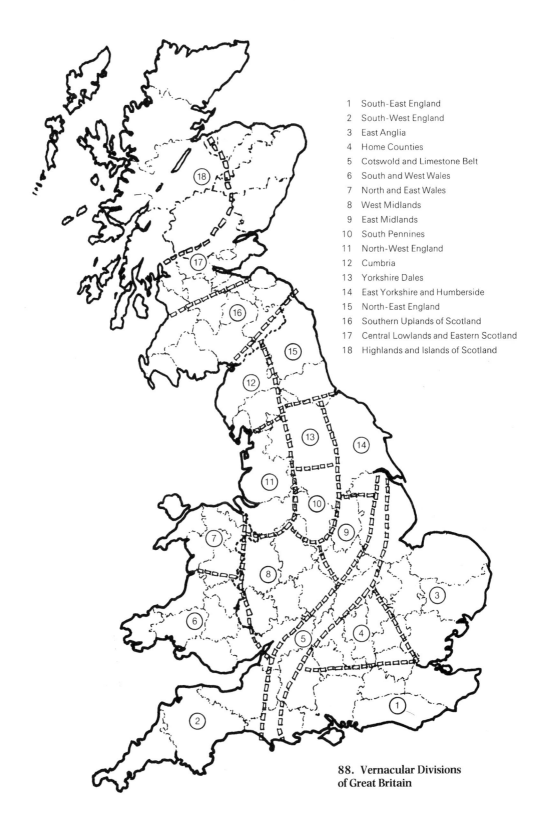

1   South-East England
2   South-West England
3   East Anglia
4   Home Counties
5   Cotswold and Limestone Belt
6   South and West Wales
7   North and East Wales
8   West Midlands
9   East Midlands
10 South Pennines
11 North-West England
12 Cumbria
13 Yorkshire Dales
14 East Yorkshire and Humberside
15 North-East England
16 Southern Uplands of Scotland
17 Central Lowlands and Eastern Scotland
18 Highlands and Islands of Scotland

**88. Vernacular Divisions
of Great Britain**

The South-East of England

89. Fairfield, Eastry, Kent
This house, which may be early fifteenth-century in date, has a central hall and flanking wings, one wider than the other. The hall is aisled and the dormer indicates that an intermediate floor has been inserted. The hall fireplace appears to back onto a cross-passage. The wings are jettied in two directions. The mixture of wall-cladding materials is not unusual in Kent.

90. Typical vernacular buildings and details from South-East England

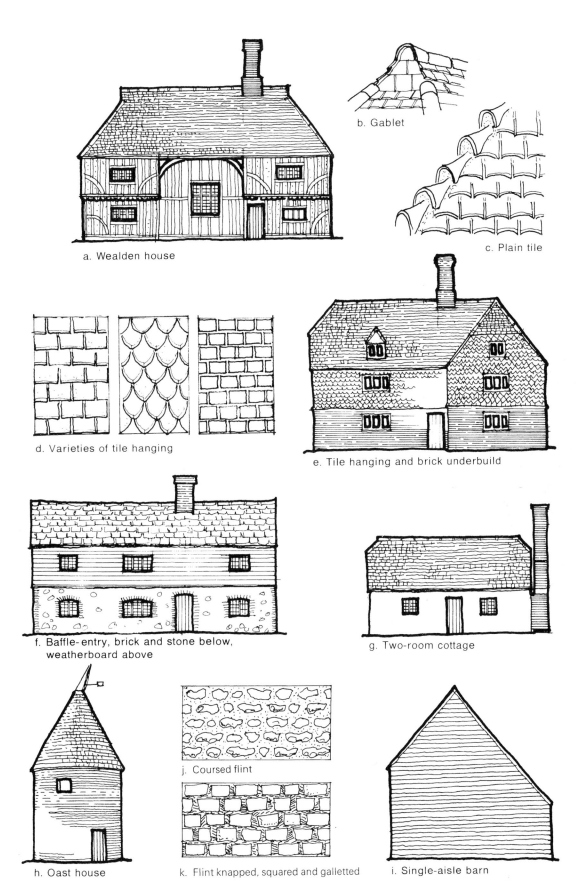

a. Wealden house

b. Gablet

c. Plain tile

d. Varieties of tile hanging

e. Tile hanging and brick underbuild

f. Baffle-entry, brick and stone below, weatherboard above

g. Two-room cottage

h. Oast house

j. Coursed flint

k. Flint knapped, squared and galletted

i. Single-aisle barn

The South-West of England

91. Inn at South Zeal, Devon
The cob-walled and thatched building has a porch at the position of the original cross-passage. The tarred base to the wall and the neat thatch to the roof, gently swept around the porch, are characteristic of the region.

92. Typical vernacular buildings and details from South-West England

a. Longhouse of granite and thatch

e. Cottage, slate-hung upper floor

b. Cob and thatch

f. Ash-house

c. Cob, thatch and front chimney

g. Elongated chapel

d. Cob over stone

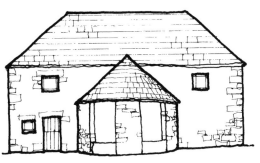

h. Barn and horse-engine house

East Anglia

93. House at Swaffham Bulbeck, Cambridgeshire This house has the baffle-entry plan found so frequently in the eastern counties of England. The timber-frame has close studding and the thatch comes to pointed gables, both also regional characteristics. The main part of the building has been divided into two and the portion on the extreme right appears to be an addition, structurally separate from the rest though under the same roof.

94. Typical vernacular buildings and details from East Anglia

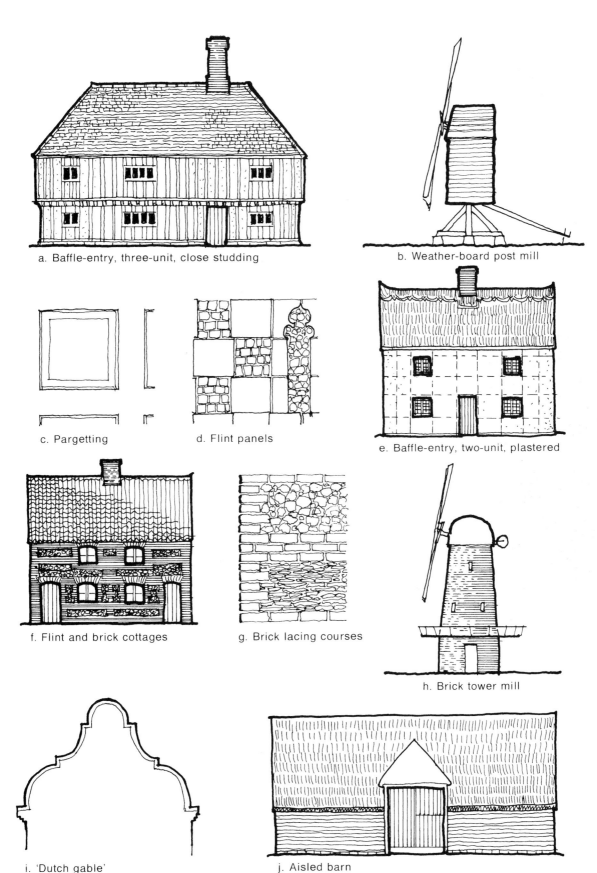

a. Baffle-entry, three-unit, close studding

b. Weather-board post mill

c. Pargetting

d. Flint panels

e. Baffle-entry, two-unit, plastered

f. Flint and brick cottages

g. Brick lacing courses

h. Brick tower mill

i. 'Dutch gable'

j. Aisled barn

The Home Counties

95. House at Longworth, Berkshire
Many plan-types and many building materials are found in the Home Counties to the West and North of London. This house, of two rooms on each floor and a central entrance, has rendering over walls which are probably of a soft, chalky stone. Thin stone tiles cover the roof. The house is dated 1783.

96. Typical vernacular buildings and details from the Home Counties

a. Altered Wealden house, close studding

b. Baffle-entry, part brick,
part weather-board

c. Plaster and thatch baffle-entry

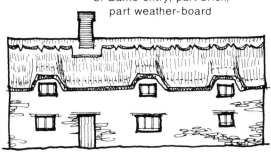

d. Stone and thatch baffle-entry, three-units

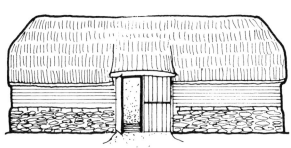

e. Thatched barn, weather-board over stone

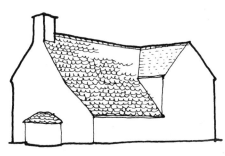

f. Outshut, oven projection

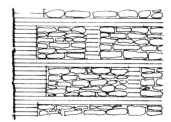

g. Poor stone, brick lacing

h. Late timber-frame

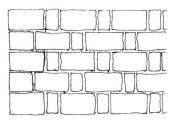

i. Rat trap bond – bricks on edge

j. Earth-walled cottage

k. Stone cottage

l. Late timber-frame cottages

The Cotswolds and the Limestone Belt

97. Farmhouse at Aston-sub-Edge, Gloucestershire Dated 1631, the house has ashlar walls to the ground floor and a gable wall with timber-framed walls to the first floor on the long elevation. The mullioned windows with label moulds are prominent in the gable wall while the timber-framing includes closely-spaced studs and long straight braces at each end. The tall, square grouped chimney stacks are of a type common in the Cotswolds.

98. Typical vernacular buildings and details from the Cotswolds and the Limestone Belt

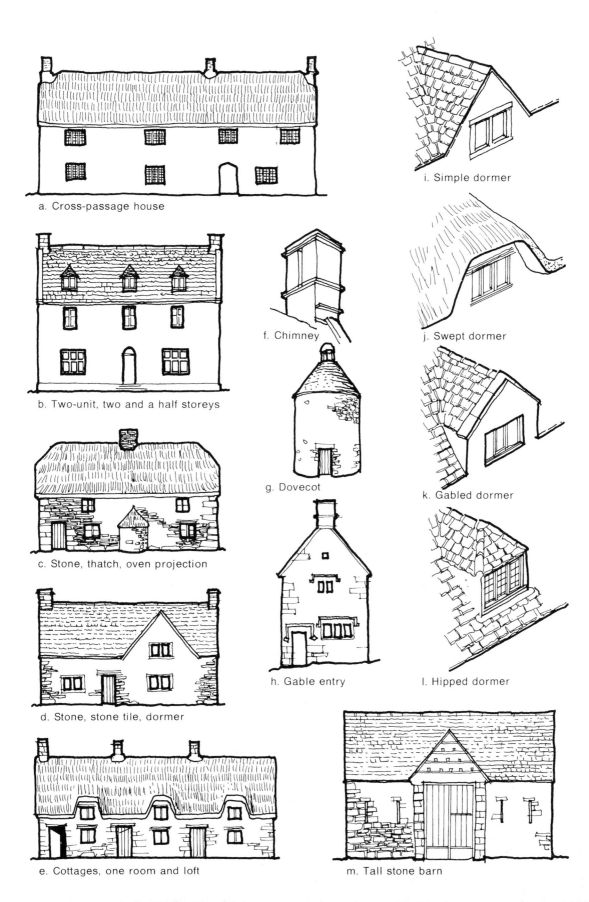

a. Cross-passage house

b. Two-unit, two and a half storeys

c. Stone, thatch, oven projection

d. Stone, stone tile, dormer

e. Cottages, one room and loft

f. Chimney

g. Dovecot

h. Gable entry

i. Simple dormer

j. Swept dormer

k. Gabled dormer

l. Hipped dormer

m. Tall stone barn

South and West Wales

99. House at Merthyr Cynog, Breconshire (now Powys)
This house and its attached farm buildings are from the hills just outside Brecon. The walls are of a rough stone much improved from many layers of whitewash and the roof has a steep pitch intended for thatch but re-roofed in slate from North Wales. The dormers are recent though the house was probably built with loft spaces. The chimney stacks are squat and heavy.

100. Typical examples of vernacular buildings and details from South and West Wales
Includes the cross-passage houses of the south-east, the front chimney houses of Pembrokeshire, and the whitewashed and thatched houses of the Vale of Glamorgan.

a. Whitewashed stone house, attached cow-house

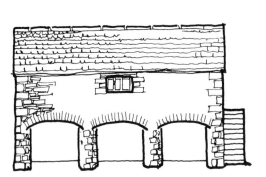

b. Granary over cartshed

c. Front chimney stack

d. Thatched and whitewashed, back-to-back fireplace

e. Stone cottages, brick dressings

f. Clay and thatch cottage

g. Cow-house, loft over

h. Stone chapel

North and East Wales

101. Haybarn from Maentwrog, Merionethshire (now Gwynedd)
This haybarn is typical of Snowdonia in having posts made of solid piers of slate. In the foreground there is the gable of a field barn built at right angles to the slope.

102. Typical examples of vernacular buildings and details from North and East Wales
The timber-frame and stone areas near the English border and the areas of hard stones and blue slates in North-West Wales.

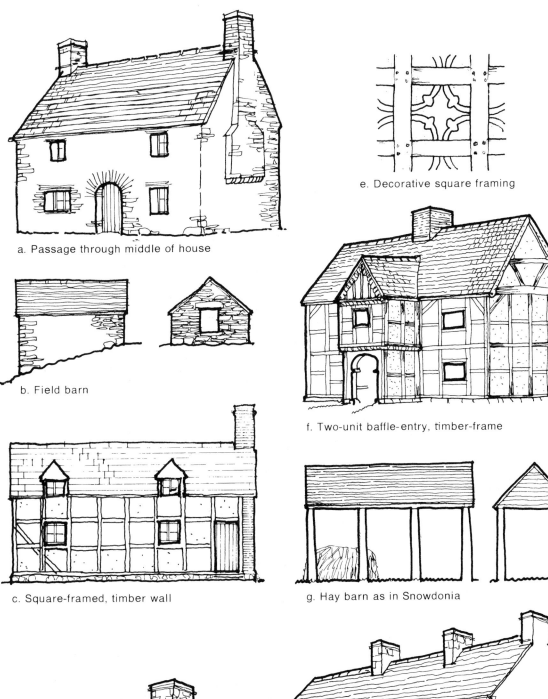

a. Passage through middle of house

b. Field barn

c. Square-framed, timber wall

d. Cottage with loft at one end

e. Decorative square framing

f. Two-unit baffle-entry, timber-frame

g. Hay barn as in Snowdonia

h. Quarrymen's cottages

The West Midlands

103. House at Brampton Bryan, Herefordshire
This house has the half-timbering with square panels which is so characteristic of the West Midlands. The prominent chimney breast projecting from the gable wall is also characteristic though the chimney stacks appear to have been rebuilt in brickwork. The steeply pitched roof is now slated but would have been designed for thatch with tiny first floor windows tucked under a deep eaves.

104. Typical vernacular buildings and details from the West Midlands

a. Jettied timber-frame

b. Hall and cross-wing

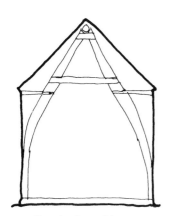
c. Crucks in gable

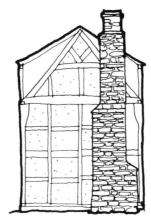
d. Box-frame, gable roof raised

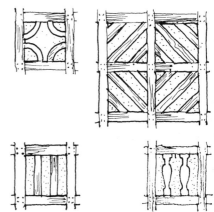
e. Decorated panelling

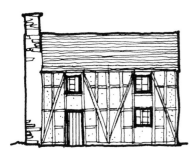
f. Late timber-framing

g. Cottage, one and a half room

h. One-room cottage

i. Town terrace, timber-frame and brick

The East Midlands

105. Houses at Hoby, Leicestershire

The brick house appears to be of 'baffle-entry' plan. It has a 'plat band' between the two storeys and 'dentillated brickwork' at the eaves. When first built the roof was probably of thatch held between the gable parapets. The house to the right has a jettied first floor and is presumably timber-framed. To the left another brick house hides its roof behind a parapet.

106. Typical vernacular buildings and details from the East Midlands

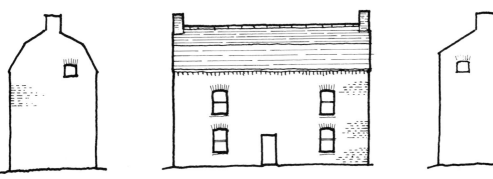

a. Typical brick house of two storeys with tall garret space

b. Baffle-entry, one and a half storey

c. 'Mud-walled' cottages

d. Gabled projections at rear

e. Hall and brick cross-wing

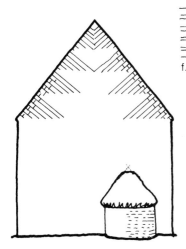

h. 'Tumbled-in' brick gable, oven projection

f. Flemish stretcher bond

g. Flemish garden wall bond

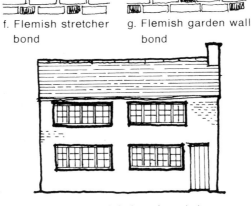

i. Framework knitters' workshop

j. Loomshop over cottage

The Southern Pennines

107. Longfield House, Heptonstall, Yorkshire, W.R.
This house, severe in its darkened gritstone, is of a double-pile plan. Its pedimented doorway suggests an early eighteenth-century date, but the mullioned and transomed windows are conservative while the huge window range to the right of the doorway is quite archaic.

108. Typical vernacular buildings and details from the Southern Pennines including the Peak District

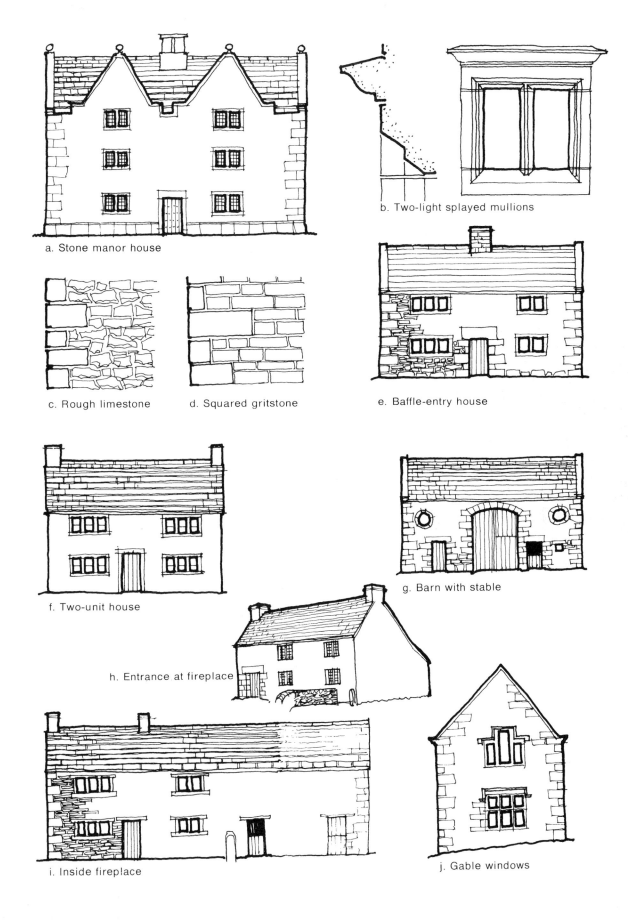

a. Stone manor house

b. Two-light splayed mullions

c. Rough limestone

d. Squared gritstone

e. Baffle-entry house

f. Two-unit house

g. Barn with stable

h. Entrance at fireplace

i. Inside fireplace

j. Gable windows

The North-West of England

109. Chorley Hall, Alderley Edge, Cheshire
Here are combined in one house two of the building materials which are so characteristic of Lancashire and Cheshire: timber-frame with small decorative panels, and sandstone easily worked into moulded dressings.

The roof of heavy gritstone flags is also characteristic of the North-West.

110. Typical vernacular buildings and details of the north-western counties of Lancashire and Cheshire

154

a. Baffle-entry, three units

b. Cruck gable

c. Decorated panels

d. Daubed cruck-framed house

e. Entry at fireplace

f. Brick, two units

g. Gable entrance

h. Aisled barn

i. Cow-house at end of barn

j. Weavers' windows

k. Cellar workshop

l. Gritstone walling

Cumbria

111. Petty Hall, Orton, Westmorland (now Cumbria)
Situated just outside the Lake District proper, Petty Hall has carboniferous limestone walls and a roof of Lake District slate. Although quite a substantial house in regional terms it does not disdain the attached farm buildings but the rendered and colourwashed walls of the house distinguish the domestic from the agricultural parts. It is dated 1604.

112. Typical vernacular buildings and details of the former counties of Cumberland, Westmorland and Lancashire—North-of-the-Sands

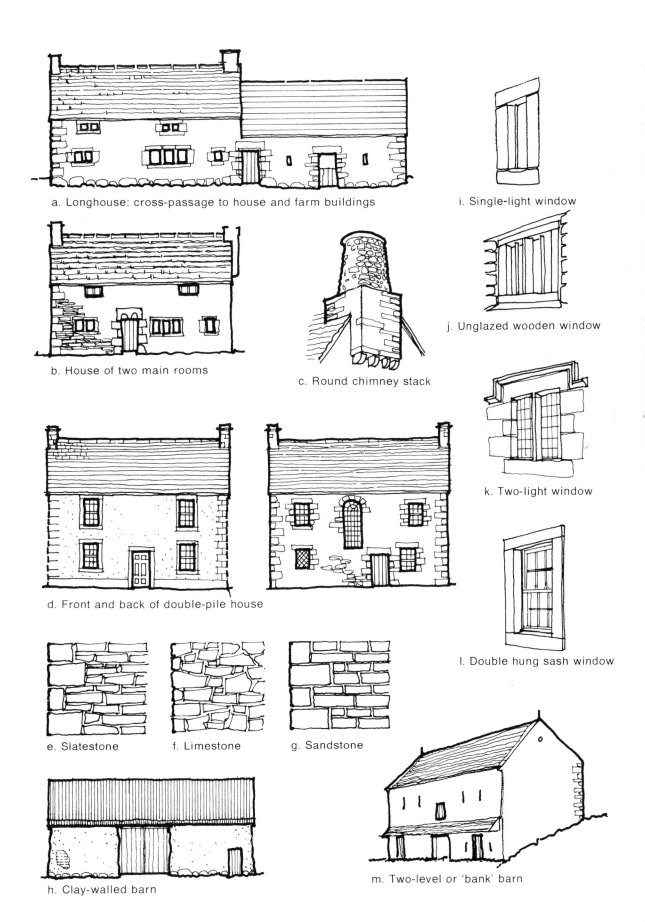

a. Longhouse: cross-passage to house and farm buildings

b. House of two main rooms

c. Round chimney stack

d. Front and back of double-pile house

e. Slatestone

f. Limestone

g. Sandstone

h. Clay-walled barn

i. Single-light window

j. Unglazed wooden window

k. Two-light window

l. Double hung sash window

m. Two-level or 'bank' barn

The Yorkshire Dales

113. House at Buttersett in Wensleydale, Yorkshire
This farmhouse is set between a cottage and farm buildings. There are two main rooms on each floor and no cross-passage. The plain sandstone walls, flagstone roofs and limited architectural decoration all contribute to the dour character of buildings in the Dales.

114. Typical vernacular buildings and details from the Yorkshire Dales

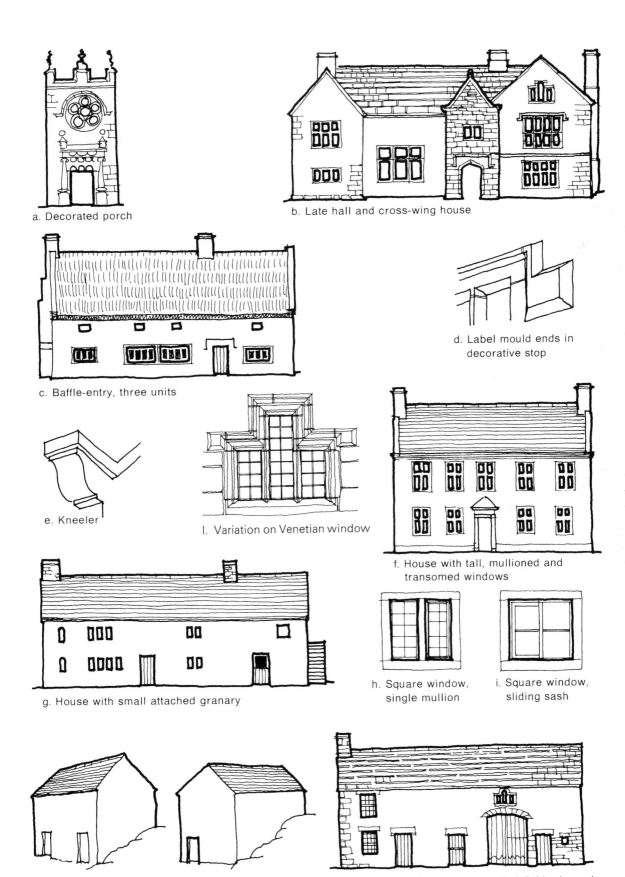

a. Decorated porch

b. Late hall and cross-wing house

c. Baffle-entry, three units

d. Label mould ends in decorative stop

e. Kneeler

l. Variation on Venetian window

f. House with tall, mullioned and transomed windows

g. House with small attached granary

h. Square window, single mullion

i. Square window, sliding sash

j. Field barn

k. Combined house and barn called 'laithe house'

East Yorkshire and Humberside

115. House at Hovingham, Yorkshire, N.R.
Located in the north-east part of Yorkshire, the village of Hovingham glows with white magnesian limestone walls under red pantiled roofs.

116. Typical vernacular buildings and details from East Yorkshire including the vale of York, Cleveland and Humberside

a. Baffle-entry, two-unit, brick and pantile

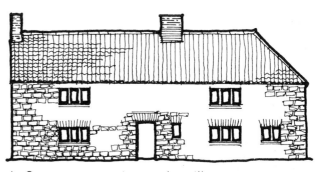

b. Cross-passage, stone and pantile

c. Cross-passage, whitewashed stone

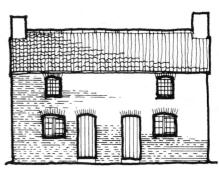

d. Cottages, brick and pantile

e. Collar purlin roof exposed in gable

f. Cross-passage house, former open hall

g. Double-pile house, extra bay housing labourers at one end

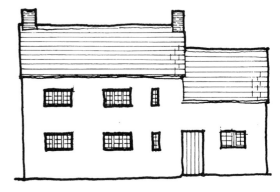

h. Cross-passage serving scullery

The North-East of England

117. Tower-house at Long Horsley, Northumberland
This grim tower-house reminds us that until fairly recently vernacular architecture in the Border region was confined to defensible Large Houses and rather flimsy almost disposable Small Houses, cottages and farm buildings. The mullioned and transomed windows date from the period after defence had been a major factor in design.

118. Typical vernacular buildings and details from the north-eastern counties of Northumberland and Durham

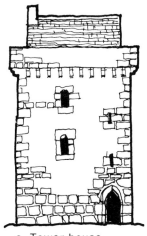

a. Tower house

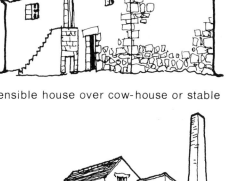

b. Bastle house, i.e. defensible house over cow-house or stable

h. Remains of leadworks

c. Rendered stone and pantile

d. Pair of cottages, one room and a loft

i. House approached via passage

e. Miner's cottage

j. House with attached barn etc

f. Cartshed under granary

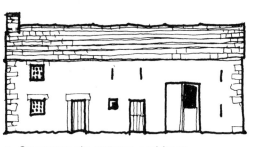

g. Quarryman's cottage and barn

The Southern Uplands of Scotland

119. Amisfield Tower, Dumfriesshire
This imposing tower house has rubble walls with dressed quoins and it has relieving arches above windows and doorway. The bulge and rounded corner on the right indicates the position of a winding staircase connecting all floors above the basement level. The skyline is enlivened by turrets and watch-tower as well as by the crow-stepped gables.

120. Typical vernacular buildings and details from the Southern Uplands of Scotland

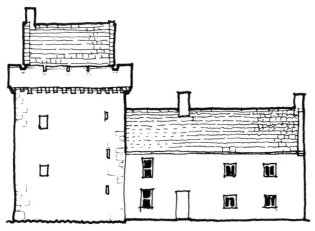

a. Tower house, much later extension

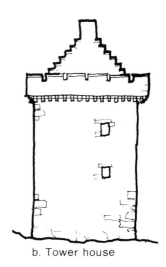

b. Tower house

c. Two room, single-storey cottage

d. Tall town house

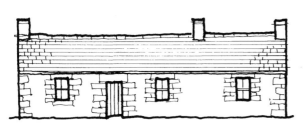

e. Three room, single-storey cottage

g. One and a half storey house

f. Cottage with five-sided dormers

h. Cottage with dormers

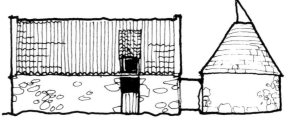

i. Barn and kiln

The Central Lowlands of Scotland

121. House at Dunblane, Perthshire
This building displays the external staircase and first floor entrance which survives sometimes in Scottish town houses. The characteristic 'harling' of the wall surface sets off the painted stone dressings in a pleasingly decorative manner.

122. Typical vernacular buildings and details from the Central Lowlands of Scotland

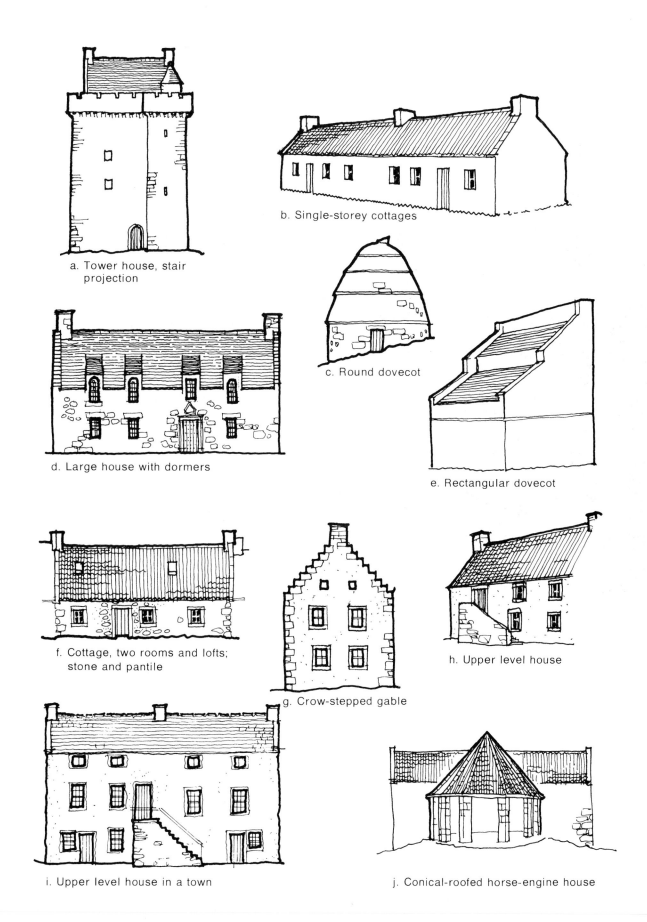

a. Tower house, stair projection

b. Single-storey cottages

c. Round dovecot

d. Large house with dormers

e. Rectangular dovecot

f. Cottage, two rooms and lofts; stone and pantile

g. Crow-stepped gable

h. Upper level house

i. Upper level house in a town

j. Conical-roofed horse-engine house

The Highlands and Islands of Scotland

123. Houses at Cromarty, Black Isle, Ross and Cromarty
The small single-storey house in the foreground is typical of so many of the late-eighteenth and early-nineteenth-century houses in the region. The large double-pile house in the background has a boldly-projecting chimney breast tapering from ground and first-floor fireplaces to rather squat chimney stacks.

124. Typical vernacular buildings and details of the Highlands and Islands of Northern Scotland

a. Two-roomed cottage, rough stone and turf, heather thatch

c. Large but late tower house

b. Cottage, two rooms, stone and thatch

d. Large house, rendered stone

e. Cottage, two rooms and loft

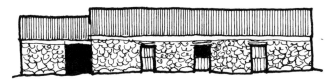

f. Croft group in islands

g. One and a half storey house

h. Farmhouse and U-shaped buildings

i. Cow-house

j. Barn and kiln

Chapter 10

How do we go deeper into the subject?

This book is only an introduction. It cannot hope to provide more than the first few steps towards a subject which is becoming more and more clear, more and more well defined as study broadens and deepens. Although the term 'vernacular architecture' may have been in use for over 140 years, serious study of the subject as we now understand it has only been conducted for little more than half that period, and study at anything like the present intensity is scarcely a generation old. Of the students of the subject nearly all have been amateurs, coming from some allied field but still amateurs in the best sense of that misused word; even now there are very few professionals and their work is partly based upon and considerably supported by the growing body of enthusiastic amateurs.

Fortunately, most of the amateurs work at a professional rather than an amateurish level. They realise that for work to be valuable as well as satisfying it must be done in a systematic manner. Every student, amateur or professional, builds on the work of his colleagues and predecessors, confident that their work is as reliable, as well-founded as his own. Although this book is only an introduction it is hoped that hints towards systematic study have already been provided for those who want to take the subject a stage further, for one can proceed by developing theoretical studies, studies in siting and location, studies in planning and design, studies in construction and materials, studies in detailing and decoration, studies in individual buildings, studies in regional character. Those so inclined can make deeper studies of any one of these sections of the subject, others can choose to make wider but shallower studies, developing several aspects of the subject simultaneously.

The term 'theoretical studies' is probably too pretentious but it is meant to suggest the study of the way in which people thought about the designs for their buildings, why they took certain courses, what was the background to their choice, how did their procedures develop into the ones with which we are familiar today. Such studies impinge onto many other subjects from philosophy to family life. They will help us all the better to see the wood while some of us choose to concentrate on the trees.

Studies of siting and location help to relate vernacular architecture to wider aspects particularly of geography and economic history. We know very well that nowadays the choice of a house involves a compromise between many different factors: the house must be near the office or the railway station, near the shops and near the schools, with a compact easily-run garden but not overlooked by neighbours, near the heart of things but with easy access to the seaside and countryside, near to a motorway but without motorway noise, with plenty of choice of employment but far from factories or tall office blocks. We understand only too well that most features are incompatible with each other

125. House in Hare Street, Hertfordshire

This house appears to have a rectangular ground plan with a jettied upper storey at one end giving the effect of a cross-wing. The position of the chimney stack (which also lies forward of the ridge) suggests an inserted fireplace related to a cross-passage. The bay at the right-hand side may have been two-storey from an early date. The dormer window suggests that an open hall was divided by an inserted floor. The half-hipped roof is quite common in the Wealden tradition. The walls have closely-spaced timber studs and there is one curved brace in the projecting upper storey.

Although not a Wealden house the building is in the tradition of south-eastern England even though actually located in Hertfordshire.

171

and so we accept that we must make the best possible compromise. Our predecessors also had to compromise but we know little enough about what the factors were in siting and location which they considered important. They needed water but how important was it to avoid unhealthy waterlogged ground? They farmed in strips but how did the shape and position of their fields of strips determine the land available for building? They needed timber for houses but what was the relative importance of the need for timber for fuel? We like to build on flat or gently sloping land; was such land too valuable to our ancestors to waste on mere house construction?

We are accustomed to the rooms and their uses in our own houses, in the ways in which cattle and pigs are housed nowadays, in the requirements for even the simplest industrial processes. But this does not mean that our ancestors regarded the same planning problems with anything like the same attitudes. Nowadays we tend to segregate room uses very considerably, we do not expect to have to watch television or entertain honoured guests in the same room in which we cook the bacon though we do expect to peel the potatoes in the same room in which we boil them. Having only a single source of heat, as often as not, did our seventeenth century predecessors look at things in the same way? They might boil the potatoes on the single hearth but did they peel the potatoes there or outside? What labels should we apply to the rooms which we can see in early buildings?

Although we now have a large and growing collection of plans of vernacular buildings we still have some distance to go in understanding the basis for planning of houses and other simple buildings of the past.

Even in constructional matters there are many avenues to explore. It is now appreciated that techniques of timber jointing were not static but developed over many centuries. Different ways of bonding bricks together for stability or good appearance are being discovered. What is there still to be discovered about building in flint or clay, roofing in slate or tiles? Even now, sixty years after the first crude map of the distribution of cruck construction was published, and in spite of the recent preparation of a comprehensive catalogue of crucks, examples of the technique are constantly being discovered and sometimes in the most unlikely places. How many more still await discovery?

It may reasonably be assumed that study of architectural decoration can be firmly based on the painstaking measurement of mouldings in churches and cathedrals by the architects of the Gothic Revival in the nineteenth century. But how carefully did the vernacular masons follow the precedent of these superior buildings? What was the reason for the extraordinary affection of builders in the Pennines for the use of the mullion centuries after it had been abandoned elsewhere? How many cottages and farmhouses, let alone barns and mills used standard doorways and window surrounds made in a sort of mass production, or at least batch production, and bought by the half dozen to be incorporated in a bit of 'do-it-yourself' walling? A great deal of work still has to be done on such matters.

While the broad basis for regional character may be now quite well appreciated there are countless sub-regional variations which one suspects are still waiting for definition. The design guides prepared by county planning authorities are sometimes criticised for being kept too strictly to local

126. Almshouses

This is a row of cottages with the ground floor set back behind an open arcade. The date, 1637, which appears on a plaque above the entrance, is early for cottages but this date and the composition based on the set of arches contained within a continuous label mould show that these cottages are in a special category and they are, in fact, almshouses. As such they might be considered as beyond the vernacular range. But a local granite is used in huge blocks for the walls, the roof is thatched, and the architectural decoration gives a rude and powerful version of the Renaissance rather than one refined and correct according to the rules of architectural grammar. So the building may reasonably be described as being vernacular.

The combination of granite and thatch suggests a location in the South-West and the almshouses are actually to be found at Moretonhampstead in Devon.

127. Manor House

This is clearly a Large House rather than an ordinary farmhouse. Apart from the wing at the right it has a symmetrical elevation with a plan based, as the central chimney stack shows, on a lobby entrance, and it has a tall, multi-storey porch to mark the entrance. The walls are of very good quality stone and the roof is of stone tiles laid to a steep pitch. The windows are mullioned but are based on the shape of a square divided by a single mullion and the wider ranges of windows consist of pairs of these squares with a more elaborate 'king mullion' in between. This window shape, the use of hipped dormer windows and the type of decoration on the chimney stacks shows Renaissance influence.

The combination of fine stone walls, steep-pitched roof, stone tile roof covering and tentative Renaissance detailing suggest that the house comes from the Limestone Belt and it is from Weldon, in Northamptonshire, towards the northern end of the region.

government boundaries which now, and especially since the recent change from some of the traditional boundary lines, may have little relation to the true limits of the regional and district traditions whose effects they are trying to perpetuate.

All these topics and many more cry out for systematic study which should involve a combination of fieldwork and library work: fieldwork because the buildings are our principal documents, they provide most of our evidence, library work because the records give us the basis for interpretation of the objects studied in the field, they tell us what the mute stones cannot explain. The techniques of fieldwork have been developed over many years and have benefitted from developments in other fields. Generally fieldwork involves some combination of extensive and intensive study: the one seeks to collect a limited amount of information from a large number of examples, the other seeks to extract a large amount of information from a small number of examples. One student may spend six months in the superficial survey of 6000 examples, another may spend the same period in the minute examination of only one building. The techniques of library work are also well established. Some involve the documentary equivalent of extensive surveys, the use of large collections of material (such as census returns) from which only limited items of information are relevant and will be used; others involve the equivalent of intensive surveys, careful transcription of small numbers of difficult documents full of pertinent facts.

The study is of interest and value to the individual student as it is conducted and drawn to a convincing conclusion but left in that state it is of no use to anyone else. A study written up and published or deposited in an archive benefits both student and community. The amateur is understandably reluctant to commit his results to paper for possible criticism but a careful and systematic report on an investigation makes the study complete.

The books listed in the bibliography will help anyone interested to take the subject a stage further. Some concentrate on planning or construction, others relate to specific buildings types, others again are devoted to fieldwork procedures. Further work can easily be done by an individual working alone. But much of the best of the recent work in the field of vernacular architecture has been done by groups, pooling resources, maintaining enthusiasm and, through criticism, providing a curb to the wilder speculations. A number of comprehensive village studies have been undertaken. A group will prepare measured surveys of all the vernacular buildings in the village, achieve a balance of the fieldwork with oral and documentary studies and then prepare a report suitable for publication. These village studies have usually begun as classes run by the Extra-Mural Department of the local university or by the Workers Educational Association. Such courses are advertised in the publications of these bodies; if one is not available for a particular locality then enough requests will encourage the organisers to build on the latent enthusiasm and provide a course. For the individual who would like to discover more about what is involved before embarking on a survey there are summer schools and week-end courses run by various universities, field study centres, residential further education establishments of local authorities. Most counties have such centres, many are in very attractive parts of the country and can provide opportunities for practice in fieldwork as well as lectures. Many county or district historical or archaeological societies include sections devoted to these studies. Often they learn about vernacular buildings of interest or under threat through the statutory procedures for notification of proposed demolition of listed buildings. Often such a group can ensure the preservation of such buildings by revealing unsuspected items of interest to the owners or proving exceptional architectural or historical interest of the buildings to the authorities. Nationally the study of vernacular architecture is fostered by the Vernacular Architecture Group through its meetings, publications and through the affiliated societies which exist in many parts of the country.

How can we find out more about houses or other buildings from books and documents? Well, some sources of information tell about buildings in general, others tell about the forms taken by buildings and others again tell of the names and occupations of the inhabitants of houses, while some give plans and even descriptions of actual structures.

General understanding of what can be applied to specific buildings should come from the developing study of vernacular architecture as represented by the books recommended for further reading and the works in their bibliographies, but two other sources are worth specific mention. One is the architectural pattern books published from the early eighteenth century. Some were directed at tradesmen giving details of labours and prices in building construction, but also giving architectural or constructional details sometimes; an example is *The Builder's Jewel* by Batty and Thomas Langley which appeared in 1741 though with many later editions. Others were books of designs, mainly for large or pretentious buildings, but sometimes including designs for farmhouses and farm buildings. While polite rather than vernacular both types included drawings which were adapted for use in smaller buildings of the late eighteenth and early nineteenth centuries. The other source lies in travellers' descriptions. The observations of Celia Fiennes on her accommodation during one journey have already been mentioned and the description by Daniel Defoe of the textile workers' cottages in the Halifax area is well-known, but sometimes more detailed descriptions may be found as in John Stow's *Survey of London* of 1598.

The layout of farmsteads, the relationship of farmhouses to farm buildings, the location of a watermill to its power source are all of interest in general and more specifically. These appear in maps and plans. Early estate maps do not usually show individual buildings, though when they do, as in the Kingston map illustrated in the Royal Commission for Historic Monuments in England's *Inventory* for West Cambridgeshire and dated 1720, they may be colourful and picturesque. Estate surveys were of course made from time to time, as on a change of ownership, for example, and the maps accompanying the written survey can be quite informative. Maps of many towns from increasingly accurate surveys were published in the eighteenth and nineteenth centuries; they followed on from the decorative, but diagrammatic bird's-eye views published, for instance, with John Speed's county maps of 1611–12.

By the Tithe Commutation Act of 1836 all land subject to tithe in England and Wales was surveyed and maps and commentaries were prepared. Most date from about 1836–1850. The maps show buildings, fields with boundaries and names, roads, water courses etc., and the schedules list owners, occupiers of the land, together with crops grown in the fields. Not all the countryside was subject to tithe which had been commuted in many parishes, perhaps at the time of enclosures, but where available in the County Record Office the tithe map is a very good and detailed indicator of the state of a piece of countryside and its building in the early nineteenth century.

The most reliable and comprehensive maps, of course, are the Ordnance Survey maps which began with William Roy's Great Map of Scotland, prepared for military purposes in 1747–55 following the Jacobite Rebellion of 1745. The Ordnance Survey extended to England, Wales and Ireland with the publication of maps of the whole country to the familiar 1:63360 or 1 inch to one mile scale. The series has been republished and copies are easily available. The 1:10560 or 6 inches to one mile series was published in the 1840s with revisions towards the end of the nineteenth century and again early in the twentieth century. These maps show field boundaries and individual buildings. The 1:2500 or 25-inch series prepared for most of the country from 1853 is even more detailed and is the most generally available source for the block plans of urban buildings. However, some towns were surveyed to even larger scales and included the actual floor plans of some of the most important buildings. In Cheshire, for instance, 10 towns were mapped to 1:500 scale. Current Ordnance Survey maps are usually kept in Town Planning or Building Surveyor's Departments, but the older maps are kept in the Library or Record Office.

If we want to find out what kind of person occupied a house or used some other building, and if we hope that the name of a person will provide the key to unlock other sources we need a census or directory. The obvious source is the National Census. The first was made in England and Wales in 1801, though only very limited information was collected, and the most useful are those prepared at ten-year intervals from 1841—the 1901 material has now become available. Inhabitants are listed dwelling by dwelling and street by street in a parish or ward, and so the density of occupation of a house as well as many long-forgotten occupations (such as mantua-maker) can be determined from the census. The original records are kept in the Public Record Office in Kew, Surrey, but local public libraries usually keep the copies pertaining to their localities.

For periods before 1841 limited information can be extracted from other sources. Commercial directories, such as Kelly's Directories, were published for counties and towns and include names and addresses and sometimes occupations also. Central government taxation records may be useful: the Hearth Tax Returns for England and Wales of 1662–89 list the names of those paying the tax (and the number of hearths for which tax was paid) parish by parish, but names are not linked to addresses nor is there any means of identifying a dwelling, and the substantial numbers of poor persons excused the tax are not listed at all; similarly the Window Tax levied from 1695 to 1851 can provide only limited information.

As has already been mentioned, the vast range of sale particulars, both those published in newspapers and those prepared for auction or private treaty sale, may be searched. No doubt much of such ephemera has been lost, but local newspapers are usually available on microfilm in public libraries and some County Record Offices have been able to acquire the archives of estate agents or solicitors. This material is especially useful for early vernacular industrial buildings where the textile machinery, for instance, was sold with the building.

Title deeds to properties are rarely of much help in studying the buildings. The deeds relate to land rather than the buildings on the land and most deeds currently available only take back the title to a recent point, perhaps when the land was first included in the Land Register. Leases may contain more useful information, perhaps including a specification of the building which had to be erected on the land leased. Wills are not often of much help in determining the form of a building though provisions (such as specifying rooms and kitchen privileges reserved for a widow) may indicate internal subdivision of a house and shed some light on the way it was used. However, as already noted, the inventory of the goods and chattels belonging to the deceased and included with the will may be illuminating in showing the number of rooms and their contents and so the way of life they served. Detailed inventories generally survive from the period c1670 to c1740. Until 1858 wills were proved by diocesan authorities and some may still remain in diocesan record offices though most have gradually been moved to the County Record Office.

Description of parsonage houses owned by the Church of England are given in the 'terriers' which were first prepared in 1571, though most date from after 1660. Comments on the accommodation and the state of repair were made after regular visitations and the history of present and former rectories and vicarages can be traced through these records.

Other descriptions of certain properties may be found in local government records. As well as the buildings owned by such authorities the local archives may contain descriptions of buildings such as cottages inspected under the Public Health Acts with a view to improvement or closure. Local authorities also have acquired over the years many properties in connection with civic improvements, such as road widening, which for one reason or another have not taken place and details of these properties may be interesting.

For buildings on land belonging to the great estates the estate records can provide descriptions and accounts of repairs or rebuilding over the years. Such estates include those of the landed gentry, but also of corporate bodies such as the Oxford and Cambridge Colleges or the trustees of charities, such as Greenwich Hospital, which have owned vast territories over several centuries. Where available these estate records can tell a great deal about buildings still in estate hands or sold to private owners.

For descriptions of buildings of 'special architectural or historic interest' (i.e. listed buildings) the 'greenbacks' issued by the Department of the Environment are invaluable. These are the statutory lists and are arranged parish by parish in the various counties of England and also under the auspices of the Welsh and Scottish Offices for the other countries. The early lists, prepared in the 1950s, tend to be brief, giving only limited architectural descriptions of the outsides of buildings as seen from the road, for they had to be swiftly prepared, but lists undertaken as part of the re-survey of the 1980s are much more comprehensive and, for many buildings, include descriptions of rooms and internal features both decorative such as fireplaces, and structural such as roof trusses.

The 'greenbacks' should be available for consultation in the offices of the local planning authorities and in local public libraries. The lists for England, at least, have been computerised for official use. Complete sets of lists are housed in the National Monuments Records of England, Scotland and Wales. In England the NMR is now part of English Heritage and located in Swindon. In Scotland and Wales the NMRs are held in the offices of the respective Royal Commissions on Historical Monuments in Edinburgh and Aberystwyth.

Descriptions, and sometimes plans, of individual houses appear in the published *Inventories* of the three Royal Commissions. Only certain counties and towns have been recorded and published and, until fairly recently, only buildings erected before 1715 were considered 'historical' by the Royal Commissions, but when published the information is detailed and authoritative. The record cards prepared by the investigators usually contain more information than could be published and these may be consulted at the offices of the Royal Commission. The National Monuments Records include photographs of many buildings, but also some plans and descriptions. The reports prepared by voluntary bodies recording old buildings have been deposited there. The Surrey Domestic Buildings Research Group, for instance, has deposited over 3000 reports including plans and photographs of houses and barns in that county.

One final source of detailed information on individual buildings is worth mention and that is the plans deposited with local authorities for approval under building control powers. Deposit of plans became fairly general after 1858 and compulsory after 1870 and plans of existing buildings to be altered, as well as new construction, are amongst the collections. However, the various local government reorganisations and varying policies on access to these documents mean that the plans are not necessarily available for public consultation.

It must be clear from the selection given that there is an appreciable range of sources of information about vernacular buildings, but it must be equally clear that the various items of information have to be teased out of a range of depositaries. The task is demanding, but the occasional rewards can be quite exhilarating.

Vernacular buildings are still very numerous in Britain and there are ample opportunities for further study. But the threat to these buildings from neglect, from the deterioration which comes from old age, from indifference, from prejudice, is very serious. The more systematic study is undertaken the better the heritage of vernacular buildings will be understood, appreciated and preserved. It is hoped that this introduction will encourage such study.

128. Tacolneston Farmhouse, Norfolk

At first glance this appears to be a simply-designed symmetrical two-storey house with a boldly projecting porch. At second glance one sees that the porch is slightly off-centre, pulled to the right. The chimney stack on the left is decorated while that on the right is plain, suggesting a difference in status between the two halves of the building. The mullioned and transomed window to the first floor of the porch suggests an importance to this room quite out of proportion to its size and must surely have been included for external effect. Although the house seems to be basically of timber-frame and plaster construction, the brick gable walls are decorated with crow steps and return for several feet along the front. The smooth surface of the thatch is broken by a dormer window lighting an extra storey in the right-hand half of the building, while the ridge has been reinforced with a capping embellished with the criss-cross pattern of the stays.

Chapter 11

The Vernacular Revival and its consequences

Any description or explanation of the vernacular architecture of this country is often followed by a question, 'Did vernacular architecture die out?' or another question, 'Is there a vernacular architecture of the present day?' The answer to the first question is that vernacular architecture as generally understood and as defined in this book did die out, but was immediately succeeded by a revival of vernacular architecture in a new sense. The answer to the second question is that this revived style of vernacular architecture may be seen all around us and is the basis for a sort of popular or vernacular architecture of the present day. It is the architecture particularly associated with the suburbs and the New Towns and the rise of the vernacular revival occurred simultaneously with the rise of the suburbs, the New Towns, the garden villages and the garden suburbs.

Vernacular architecture, as defined in this book, declined gradually through the late eighteenth and nineteenth centuries. As the hold of Renaissance architecture became ever stronger through the eighteenth century so the Large Houses of the countryside came to be designed by professional architects specifying fashionable materials and therefore lost their vernacular characteristics, becoming works of polite architecture. As pattern books such as those by Neve, Loudon and Langley circulated among landowners and building professionals, so their recommendations—rather than tradition—governed the design of farmhouses and farm buildings in the later nineteenth century. As popular magazines such as *The Illustrated Carpenter and Builder* circulated among local builders and supplied them with type plans and, along with building construction text books, standard constructional details so even cottages came to show more evidence of professional design rather than adherence to tradition.

The use of the building materials of the locality, timber, stone, clay and brick, has been seen to govern traditional building design and construction over many centuries. Building materials are expensive to transport and economics as well as tradition tied certain walling and roofing materials to certain locations. Even a single roofing material, such as thatch, had variations in its nature and appearance according to what traditions developed in quite precisely determined locations. The development of coastwise shipping, improvement of rivers, construction of canals, improvement of roads through the turnpike system, and eventually the spread of the railways, provided a choice between inferior but local materials, such as thatch, and superior, but distantly originating materials such as slate. Stone and the brick from local brickyards continued to be used, but mass-produced bricks from sources such as Stewartby in Bedfordshire and Ruabon in North Wales were employed increasingly widely while slates from Llanberis and Blaenau Ffestiniog, and tiles from Staffordshire, superseded local materials.

Another factor was the spread of increasingly standardised building regulations.

Deposit of plans and adherance to local bye-laws was gradually introduced borough by borough, but it was the Public Health Act of 1870 which made the system uniform. Bye-laws were still passed and operated locally, but Model Bye-laws were circulated by the Department of Health and led to an ever-increasing uniformity. The bye-laws were introduced to control building in the interests of health and safety; they did not directly control house-plans or building materials, but they affected the choice of, say, room heights and walling and roofing materials as well as window sizes and proportions.

All these and other factors meant that by the closing years of the nineteenth century houses and other humble buildings were directly or indirectly subject to professional design, were built of the most economical rather than the most traditional materials of the immediate locality, were no longer backward-looking in design and construction and were of greater and greater uniformity as they were subject to more and more demanding and uniform building regulations. Vernacular architecture as generally understood in this country barely survived into the twentieth century.

The Vernacular Revival Movement in polite architecture of the last forty years of the nineteenth century and the first twenty years or so of the twentieth century was one of several movements which were ultimately derived from the Gothic Revival of the early part of the nineteenth century.

Various influences—artistic, religious, romantic and social—had fostered the Gothic Revival in which architects led by A. W. N. Pugin and campaigners led by what became the Ecclesiological Society recommended that the pagan architecture of the Greeks and Romans should no longer be sought for inspiration. Instead, the abbeys, cathedrals, great parish churches and castles and manor houses of the Gothic period in this country and abroad should be studied for inspiration and this affected the design of new religious and secular buildings including houses. 'Middle Pointed' became the recommended style.

However, later in the nineteenth century other influences modified the rigidity of the Gothic Revival. There was a romantic movement in art and literature which fostered interest in the countryside and the supposedly ideal life of ordinary people in their cottages and farmhouses. Painters and illustrators, such as Birket Foster, sought the picturesque in village scenes rather than in sublime views of great works of Man or Nature. The moral righteousness of life in the countryside helped to give an idealised view of rural life in contrast to the wickedness and cruelty of life in the expanding industrial towns or the smoke-belching mines and factories. The long-established search for Utopia was modified to produce small ideal communities such as Blaise Hamlet near Bristol, or picturesque estate villages, such as Edensor in Derbyshire. These were in contrast to the formally planned industrial communities, such as Saltaire near Bradford.

The lectures and writings of William Morris, Philip Webb and John Ruskin heavily influenced the development of the Gothic Revival into the 'Old English', the 'Domestic Revival', the 'Arts and Crafts' and the 'Vernacular Revival' phases in architecture.

The architects designing churches and country houses at this time included George Devey (1820–86), Philip Webb (1831–1915) and Richard Norman Shaw (1831–1913). Devey followed the painters in appreciating the picturesque. He was particularly fond of the rustic charm of Kent and Sussex cottages and convincingly

182

re-created the vernacular architecture of Kent while anticipating the later Vernacular Revival. He influenced Nesfield, Shaw and Voysey. Webb designed the Red House in Bexleyheath near London in 1859 for William Morris, his close friend (though Morris later moved to Kelmscott Manor in the Cotswolds). Webb also designed Standen at East Grinstead, in Sussex, in 1891, a large, rambling country house looking as if it had been built in several periods and marked by tall chimney stacks. Richard Norman Shaw, influenced by Devey, designed his early buildings in an 'Old English' style, but he subsequently worked in the Arts and Crafts and Queen Anne modes. Leyswood in Groombridge, Sussex, built by Shaw in 1868–73, was another large rambling country house, dramatically sited and displaying tile hanging above brick walls, half-timbering and tall decorated brick chimney stacks rising above massive chimney breasts. Grim's Dyke in Harrow Weald, Middlesex, build in 1870–72 was more compact and made use internally of deep inglenooks contrasting with tall, wide, bay windows. The house was altered by later owners, but still in an 'Old English' style. All these houses were large and expensive, in scale way beyond the vernacular, however humble some of the building materials. The earlier houses paved the way for the Arts and Crafts and Vernacular Revival Movements while the later houses merged with these movements.

Arts and Crafts

The Arts and Crafts Movement was very strong both in England and Wales and in the USA. It originated in a desire to return to an ideal age in which artists and craftsmen, through their guilds, used traditional tools, and techniques to work with traditional materials, especially timber and stone, to produce artefacts which exuded honesty. In contrast to the machine-based productions which dominated the exhibits in the Crystal Palace Great Exhibition of 1851 those in the Arts and Crafts Movement sought to produce the honest results of honest toil by craftsmen devoted to their crafts.

The architectural component of the Arts and Crafts Movement had similar aims. The architects realised that machine-based technology was affecting the design and construction of buildings especially through building materials. They preferred to work with the irregular bricks of the local kilns rather than the hard machine-pressed bricks of the Hoffman Kilns, produced in a uniform and predictable supply for the adjacent railway sidings. Their buildings had the half-timbered, tile-hung, brick or roughcast walls of traditional buildings of the countryside and were designed and constructed to have the pure structural integrity of traditional buildings of the past to their credit. Houses in the Arts and Crafts style were generally smaller than those of the 'Old English'; some were isolated houses in the countryside, but many were large homes for middle-class owners located on outer suburban sites. Although such houses were built quite extensively in English and Welsh counties, they were most common in the counties around London, Surrey and Hertfordshire being especially rich in examples.

Richard Norman Shaw only worked in the Arts and Crafts style for a time, but he was influential through younger architects who had worked in his office. One such was E. S. Prior (1862–1932) whose designs showed more individuality than acknowledgement to tradition, though he was careful to make use of as many local materials as he could accommodate in his designs. The Barn at Exmouth, Devon of 1895–7 and Home Place, Holt, Norfolk of 1903–5 are among his best-known

129. Sketches of nineteenth- and twentieth-century houses

a. Arts and Crafts House
based on The Barn, Exmouth, Devon, by E. S. Prior, built 1895–7, having walls of a mixture of dressed stone and local rubble. The original thatch has been replaced by local tiles.

b. Arts and Crafts House
based on Stoneywell Cottage, Ulverscroft, Leicestershire, by E. Gimson, built 1898–99 and having walls and a chimney breast which grow from an outcrop of stone. Again, the original thatch has been replaced by local tiles.

c. Vernacular Revival House
based on Deanery Gardens, Sonning, Berkshire, by Sir Edwin Lutyens and of 1901. The walls are built of small bricks and the roof of local clay tiles.

d. Vernacular Revival House
based on The Orchard, Chorleywood, Hertfordshire, built in 1900–1 by C. F. A. Voysey. The roughcast brick walls, buttresses and Lake District Slate roof are characteristic of his work.

e. Vernacular Revival Cottages
based on cottages at Apethorpe, Northamptonshire, by Sir Reginald Blomfield before 1906. The walls are of local stone and the roof is of Collyweston slates.

f. Vernacular Revival Cottages
based on designs published by A. N. Prentice in 1906; these cottages were to have brick walls roughcast above plinth level, a Lake District Slate roof and green-painted woodwork and ironwork.

g. Vernacular Revival Cottages
based on a design by M. H. Baillie Scott for Letchworth Garden City, Hertfordshire, 1905. The two cottages are unified in what was to become a very common style between two gables and with low eaves.

h. Queen Anne House
based on Temperate House Lodge, Kew Gardens, Surrey, by W. E. Nesfield and, in 1867, a very early example of that style. The carefully composed brick walls and tall decorated brick chimney stack were to become characteristic of the Queen Anne style.

i. Queen Anne House
based on an example at Northwood, Middlesex, built by A. Mitchell before 1906; the house has red brick walls and a plain tiled roof with plaster pargetting between and below the upper storey windows.

a.

b.

c.

d.

e.

f.

g.

h.

i.

works. Other architects included C. R. Ashbee (1863–1942) who worked mainly in Chelsea, and Ernest Newton (1856–1922) who designed Bullews Wood, Chislehurst, Kent in 1888 which incorporated deep projecting bays and bold chimney breasts. Another product of Shaw's office was W. R. Lethaby (1857–1931) who is better known as an author than as an architect though the large country house, Avon Tyrell, Christchurch, Hampshire of 1891 and the small country church of All Saints, Brockhampton, Herefordshire of 1901–2, are testimony to his skill. Lethaby, Newton and Prior were among the founders of the Art Workers Guild, the organisation which established the Arts and Crafts Movement.

Not all the Arts and Crafts architects were London-based. E. W. Gimson (1864–1919) worked in the Cotswolds, busy in furniture manufacture and design, though his best-known building is the remarkable Stoneywell Cottage, Ulverscroft, Leicestershire of 1898 on a Z-plan growing out of an outcrop of rock by way of an enormous stone chimney breast and massive chimney stack, a genuinely timeless building. The Chester-based architect John Douglas (1829–1911) and the Manchester-based architects Edgar Wood (1860–1935) and his partner J. H. Sellars (1861–1954) are often linked with the Arts and Crafts Movement though they are just as appropriately placed among the Vernacular Revival architects.

The Arts and Crafts Movement paved the way for the Vernacular Revival. The emphasis on integrity in choice and utilisation of building materials, the determination to return to traditional building methods applied by craftsmen who loved their work, and the emphasis on the total building from planning through construction and detailing to furnishing and decoration, all helped to focus attention on examples of vernacular architecture which would otherwise be considered outmoded and due for demolition.

The Vernacular Revival Movement

The Vernacular Revival Movement in architecture overlapped the Arts and Crafts Movement, sharing some of the same beliefs, but developing in a rather different way. The architects of the Movement sought to devise a domestic architecture which looked established, permanent, was sympathetic to the landscape and brought building and site together in an inseparable whole, the house and garden being as one. They shared with the enthusiasts of the Arts and Crafts Movement a belief in the integrity of structural organisation, the importance of a sympathetic choice of materials and skill and sensitivity in the craft of building.

Inspiration for the architects of this Movement came from the ordinary or vernacular buildings of the countryside and several of the leading architects such as Guy Dawber (1861–1938), John Douglas (1829–1911) and W. B. Sanders published sketch books based on their studies of vernacular buildings in the field. These were in addition to the earlier studies of abbeys, castles, palaces and churches in Britain and overseas which had been made from the early days of the Gothic Revival onwards.

By far the most important architect of the Vernacular Revival Movement was C. F. A. Voysey (1857–1941) and his work was widely published and much praised. He developed quite early in his career simple designs for small country houses or larger houses of the outer suburbs based on straight-forward elongated or L-shaped plans with deep inglenooks and contrasting large and small windows. His favourite materials were roughcast brick walls and Westmorland green slate

130a. and b. Two details from houses in Great Budworth, Cheshire John Douglas, the Cheshire architect, did a lot of work in Great Budworth for the Arley Estate. The window illustrated here has moulded brick mullions and small-paned leaded lights beneath a brick relieving arch. The heart shape is picked out in projecting header bricks—a variation on traditional diaper brickwork.

roofs. The lines of his houses were long and horizontal with deep eaves and roof planes sloping low towards the ground. The elevations were enlivened by gables projecting from hipped roofs. The horizontality was emphasised by long lines of small windows with leaded lights just below the eaves. Sloping buttresses at each corner countered the horizontal lines and were said to benefit the structure. Contrasting tall chimney stacks served the inglenook fireplaces.

Contrary to the Arts and Crafts architects, Voysey did not believe it necessary to follow too closely the designs and building materials of the locality and built houses in many parts of the country in the same basic style, though acknowledging Arts and Crafts principles by using local stone dressings. Yet the way in which he made his houses hug their sites, stretching terraces into gardens, meant that they seemed always to be at one with their locations in a manner which eluded some other architects no matter how closely they attempted to follow the precedent of the building materials of the locality.

Among the most appreciated of Voysey's houses were Broadleys and Moorcrag, sited opposite each other on a hillside overlooking Lake Windermere and built in 1898–9. Broadleys has an L-plan, a set of bow-fronted bays embracing the view, large windows on the garden side and ranges of small windows on the entrance side. Moorcrag has a simple rectangular plan, running across the slope, a deep roof with projecting gables and one end sweeping low down to the bottom of the site. Both have the characteristic roughcast walls and corner buttresses. However, probably the most influential of Voysey's houses was The Orchard, Chorleywood, Hertfordshire built in 1900 with a strong feeling towards symmetry with its two cross-wing gables, but with an informal though balanced placing of bands of windows.

Voysey's practice was much reduced during the First World War and he built little in the interwar years or up to his death in 1941, but the pattern of two gables with a tall roof between was adopted by the designers of small houses and semi-detached cottages for a century and more.

Although Voysey was the best known of the Vernacular Revival architects there were others whose designs have been influential. One of these was M. H. Baillie Scott (1865–1945) who delighted in open planning and carefully detailed inglenooks. The house for which he is best remembered is Blackwell at Bowness-on-

131. Broadleys, Bowness-on-Windermere, Westmorland (now Cumbria)
This house, built in 1898, is one of the most admired works of C. F. A. Voysey. The main rooms with tall bow windows face onto the lake; service rooms are in a wing on the right. The roughcast stone walls are surmounted by a Lake District Slate roof. Though with few local details the house is the epitome of the Vernacular Revival style.

Windermere with its wonderful site overlooking the lake, and its roughcast walls, stone dressings and neat chimney stacks; it is a more imposing house than the nearby Broadleys and Moorcrag, but one which also seems to belong to its site yet has no more reproduction of local architectural details than the other two. Another of the Vernacular Revival architects was the young Edwin Lutyens (1869–1944) notable also for his collaboration with the garden designer Gertrude Jekyll and for the publicity his houses and her gardens received in the new magazine *Country Life*. Lutyens was fortunate in his clients and his houses were generally bigger than those of Voysey or Scott yet they were designed in the spirit of vernacular architecture and in their boldly gabled roofs, boldly soaring chimney stacks, boldly projecting bay windows and their skilful use of brick and tile acknowledged the influence of Surrey vernacular on his early houses. Munstead Wood, Godalming, Surrey of 1896–7 was his first masterpiece; Orchards, Godalming of 1897–1900 is often quoted as his best building in the Surrey vernacular, while Deanery Gardens, Sonning, Berkshire designed in 1899 for Edward Hudson, proprietor of *Country Life*, features specially made thin bricks, white clunch and heavy oak timbers, pierces the skyline with tall, decorated chimney stacks and spreads out into a garden of intersecting axes. Lutyens later moved into the Queen Anne and Neo-Georgian styles and from country houses into monumental governmental and commercial building designs, but without his work the Vernacular Revival Movement would have been appreciably weaker.

Provincial architects adopted the Vernacular Revival with enthusiasm equal to that of their London-based contemporaries. John Douglas developed a new

Cheshire vernacular of brick and half-timbering so convincing that in whole villages, such as Great Budworth, he added new buildings to old with faultless skill. Sellars and Wood took up the dour gritstone of the Lancashire and Yorkshire Pennines to produce works of strength and conviction. Guy Dawber, in addition to his Cotswolds affection, produced in a house near Denbigh of roughcast, stone and slate a building sitting in neighbourly fashion with the local timber-frame, stone and brick vernacular. Harold Henderson designed houses in the Yorkshire Dales which were much more humble than those of Voysey or Scott, let alone Lutyens, but were every bit as convincing.

Queen Anne and Neo-Georgian

The Vernacular Revival and Arts and Crafts Movements were not the only successors to the Gothic Revival. A return to the designs of the late seventeenth and early eighteenth centuries and those of the later eighteenth century was attempted by several architects and have been called the Queen Anne and Neo-Georgian styles respectively.

Queen Anne houses were designed in a free classical manner, that is a style in which classical proportions and classical details were employed but which was without the formality or correctness that later came to be required. The brick Kew Palace, of 1631, was influential and many architects turned towards the red brick and white stone freely-designed buildings of Christopher Wren. In contrast to the long, low, ground-hugging lines of the Vernacular Revival buildings, those in the Queen Anne manner stood tall, several storeys high, often with steeply pitched roofs, chimneys grouped together, tall, generous windows with thick white-painted glazing bars contrasting with the brick walls and rubbed brick dressings. The Queen Anne style was appropriate for urban buildings and many London streets, especially in Chelsea, were developed in this style in the later years of the nineteenth century. These were not terraced houses as in eighteenth-century Bloomsbury, but rows of individual houses competing with each other in design, but harmonising in materials. However, the Queen Anne style was also appropriate for the blocks of exclusive flats which were added to the tall, narrow houses of London's urban tradition. In a way the Queen Anne was the urban counterpart to the rural Vernacular Revival.

W. E. Nesfield (1835–88) was an early and quite prolific architect employing this style. Temperate House Lodge, Kew Gardens, of 1867, a neat little building dominated by a tall ribbed chimney stack is an early but complete example of the style. Richard Norman Shaw was also an active practitioner of the Queen Anne style and Lowther Lodge, prominently sited on Kensington Gore in London shows brickwork at its best. J. J. Stevenson (1831–1908), a Scot who settled in London, designed Board Schools as well as town houses and the notable Munstead House of 1878 in the style.

The Queen Anne style was all very well, but just as the original free classical designs had been superseded by the correct Palladian buildings of the Georgian period so a Georgian Revival was the unsurprising development of the Queen Anne. Houses in this style were generally of brick, but stone counterparts may be found in the Pennines and other stone-bearing areas. They were tall, compact, often cubiform compositions, symmetrical and carefully proportioned. Cornices were correct in detail rather than deep plastered coves; doorways were set behind

132. Sketches of nineteenth- and twentieth-century houses

a. Scottish Traditional-Style House
based on a Gate Lodge to a Scottish estate by R. S. Lorimer, built before 1904. The stone walls are 'harled' (i.e., roughcast) under a slate roof.

b. Neo-Georgian House
based on The Salutation, Sandwich, Kent, built by Sir Edwin Lutyens in 1911 and with brick walls and stone dressings harking back beyond the Georgian to Wren.

c. Queen Anne Small House
of the type built in Bedford Park, London, which was begun in 1875. The ground floor is of exposed red brick, the upper floor is tile-hung and the roof has red clay tiles. The bay windows are prominent.

d. Queen Anne Cottages
typical of Bourneville, Warwickshire, which were begun in 1894. The semi-detached pair have brick walls under a tiled roof, boldly projecting bay windows, a sort of Palladian upper-floor window and a quaint dormer.

e. Interwar Suburban Houses
based on a semi-detached pair from Harrow in 'Metroland'. The brick walls are roughcast above the plinth and the roofs are tiled. There are large bow windows at ground- and first-floor levels surmounted by gables with imitation half-timber work.

f. Interwar Suburban House
The Neo-Georgian detached house is of brick with a hipped roof of plain tiles. The inspiration is Georgian rather than the Tudor of bow windows and many gables.

g. Post-war Terraced Houses
based on a design of 1955 by Tayler and Green and erected in Hales, Norfolk. No local details are specifically incorporated, but the proportions, the choice of local bricks with flared headers and the pantiled roof help the house merge with the local vernacular.

h. House of the 1990s
from Tytherington, Cheshire, has a 'cottagey' feel from its brick walls, corbelled upper floors and timbered gables.

i. Terraced Cottages of 2001
in Wilmslow, Cheshire, show variations on a uniform plan with different designs of gables, false dormer, bay windows and doorway details.

a.

b.

c.

d.

e.

f.

g.

h.

i.

porches designed according to the rules; roofs might be of a low-pitch slate retiring behind a parapet; windows had Georgian sashes with thin glazing bars. At the same time it was understood that much of the highly appreciated vernacular of the countryside was actually eighteenth-century in date and Georgian in style. The Neo-Georgian, therefore, could be as true to the local vernacular as the Vernacular Revival.

Ernest Newton (1856–1922) built many houses in the south of England in the Neo-Georgian style; Redcoat, Haslemere, Surrey of 1894–5 is a good example, and in 1903 he published a book illustrating many of his designs. Guy Dawber (1861–1938) worked mainly in the West Country and especially in the Cotswolds whose vernacular architecture he had studied and published. After about 1905 his buildings were mainly in the Neo-Georgian style and Eyford Court, Upper Slaughter, Gloucestershire of 1910 was one such house, formally planned, with symmetrical entrance and garden elevations. Lutyens designed houses as well as public and commercial buildings in the Neo-Georgian manner and his house, The Salutation, Sandwich, Kent of 1911 is an excellent example. Among provincial architects W. H. Brierley (1862–1926) of York designed many charming houses in the Neo-Georgian as well as in the Arts and Crafts manner.

The English House and the Scottish dimension

Our understanding of the rural houses of the second half of the nineteenth century is much enhanced by the exhaustive study prepared on behalf of the German government by Hermann Muthesius. His book, *Das Englische Haus*, was published in 1904 and, remarkably, was not translated into English until 1979. Muthesius wrote about and illustrated English vernacular buildings and made perceptive comments on the work of most of the principal architects practising in London and provincial towns at that time.

Scotland was supposedly out of Muthesius' remit but he did study the work of some Scottish architects of the time. Three architects are especially significant. Rowand Anderson (1834–1921) built in 1879–82 a house, Allermuir, for his own occupation, avoiding big windows and machine ornament as an example of a 'Traditional' movement in architecture in Scotland corresponding to Arts and Crafts and the Vernacular Revival in England. Anderson was more influential as a writer and educator, calling his fellow Scots to look again at the pre-industrial 'golden age' of the Scottish Renaissance. The cult of Scottish Baronial had sprinkled the glens with vast turreted piles giving status to landowners through acknowledgment of the defensive needs of their predecessors. The Traditionalist movement was different; it recalled the buildings of a favoured class of Scotsmen below the rank of the great landowners, but above the poor farmers and cottagers whose rough black houses largely disappeared in the housing revolution of the eighteenth century.

C. R. Mackintosh (1868–1928) was a remarkable individualist among architects, well known for his Glasgow School of Art and his interiors such as in the Cranston Tea Rooms in Glasgow. He was also responsible for some notable small country houses of which Hill House, Helensburgh, near Glasgow, is the best-known. Hill House, 1902, has a partly open-plan interior, but its exterior has bold massing with walls of Scottish harling, tall wings under steeply pitched roofs and cone-topped turrets like the staircase turrets of Scottish tower houses.

Unfortunately Mackintosh fell out of favour and effectively gave up architecture in 1913, living the remainder of his life as a painter in France.

The most prolific and ultimately the most influential of the three was R. S. Lorimer (1864–1929). A pupil of Anderson and with experience of working with English architects such as G. F. Bodley, Lorimer returned to Scotland where he sought inspiration in the tower houses and the small country houses of the seventeenth century. His rugged houses had slated roofs and walls of traditional harling which may have provided the inspiration for the pebble-dash technique which became popular in England. Muthesius was fall of praise for Lorimer's work, recognising his success in recapturing the charm 'of unpretentious Scottish buildings with their honest plain-ness and simple, almost rugged, massiveness'.

Suburbia

The spread of the Vernacular Revival in architecture was linked to the spread of suburbia. The design of many, probably most, typical suburban houses built in the twentieth century was related to the design of vernacular buildings of previous centuries by way of the Vernacular Revival and other movements of the late nineteenth century.

Suburbs, in the sense of houses and other buildings erected outside the borough or city walls, were not new. Every historic town had its lines of houses bordering the roads leading to the gates in the town walls. They were built because of lack of space within the walls, or as a way of avoiding the obligations of burgage plot holders or because the protection of the walls was no longer necessary, but their extent depended on the increase in population, the legal availability of building land outside the towns and the need for transport into the towns as the suburbs extended. In the later nineteenth century factors including a huge growth in population, increase in trade and industry, anxiety to be free of urban regulations and taxes as well as the sheer shortage of building land in the towns gave an impetus to the spread of suburbs, especially around London and the major industrial cities. The development of railways, omnibuses and tramway systems meant that suburbs could spread further and further from the centres of the cities on which they depended.

Two other factors influenced the development and design of the suburbs: the push of people anxious to escape the congestion and insanitary conditions of the cities and the pull of people towards the Englishman's ideal of a house in the country. The same romantic view of life in the villages and farmsteads and the same affection for the picturesque which had helped to produce the architecture of the Arts and Crafts and Vernacular Revival Movements also fostered the building of detached houses with gardens on spacious plots on the edge of cities, where a clean, healthy life free from urban smog could be sought and for a time obtained. It is hardly surprising that designs based on the Vernacular Revival country houses of architects such as Voysey, Baillie Scott and Lutyens were chosen for the newly expanding suburbs.

Garden Suburbs and Garden Cities

Spread of the suburbs was all very well but uncontrolled spread led to the danger of re-creating the very conditions which the suburban dweller had sought to escape. The design of garden suburbs and garden cities was intended to solve the problem and while neither were completely successful both influenced the growth of suburbs in the twentieth century. Both could be traced back to Bedford Park in London, built from 1875 onwards, and ultimately to the Regents Park Village development of 1811 and later. Bedford Park was a middle-class suburb developed as a planned whole to a low density of houses to the acre and with individual or semi-detached houses designed by several architects along curved roads and preserved trees. Regents Park was a more Utopian scheme with houses and cottages dispersed in a picturesque manner around the parkland. It did not develop as intended, though the villas are still occupied as private residences albeit on a rather palatial scale.

At a lower social level there were the experiments with workers' villages fostered by enlightened employers. Communities for industrial workers were often built during the nineteenth century; Ackroyden and Saltaire in Yorkshire and Styal in Cheshire are well known. They tended to be collections of houses in rows, looking much like the workers' cottages in the towns and confined to the employees of a particular firm. More relevant to the development of suburbs were the model villages of Bourneville, near Birmingham (mostly 1894–1900), Port Sunlight in Cheshire (mainly 1885 and 1910) and New Earswick in Yorkshire (begun 1902). The cottages at Bourneville were built on plots large enough to cultivate as vegetable gardens. At Port Sunlight the cottages were designed by eminent architects to echo the timber-frame and brick vernacular of the Cheshire countryside. At New Earswick the architects, Parker and Unwin, experimented with the cul-de-sac layout which reduced the burden of street costs while avoiding the narrow frontages of urban dwellings. Hampstead Garden Suburb built from 1906 onwards was not dependent on the philanthropy of any employer; it was a middle-class suburb, though cottages were built as the plan developed. Here, Parker and Unwin were able to develop their ideas on low density layout with an urban feel. Neo-Georgian was chosen for the designs rather than the Vernacular Revival expected in a more rural location.

Garden suburbs and model villages promised an improvement on uncontrolled suburban development, but the self-contained New Towns promised an alternative. Inspired by the visionary Ebenezer Howard the proposed garden cities were intended to be satellites to the big cities, connected to them by railways but separated by green belt land. Each garden city was intended to be self-contained with its own industry and shopping, educational and cultural facilities. Housing was to be at a low density, giving plenty of garden space to each dwelling, and in an informal layout retaining grass and trees. In 1903, First Garden City Limited acquired land at Letchworth in Hertfordshire linked by train to London. The 'city' developed slowly, to designs by Parker and Unwin, but was sufficiently successful for a second garden city to be planned at Welwyn, Hertfordshire after the end of the First World War, with Louis de Soissons as architect and planner. Letchworth had a variety of designs with Vernacular Revival in the ascendant, but Welwyn Garden City was laid out spaciously to Neo-Georgian designs.

After the Second World War a number of New Town Corporations were established such as Harlow, Stevenage, Bracknell and Crawley near London, Peterlee in the North-east of England and East Kilbride in Scotland. They were intended to attract industry to properly planned industrial estates and to re-house people escaping from bombed and overcrowded cities. Following the small market

a.

b.

c.

d.

133. Twentieth-century vernacular houses

a. This is an early twentieth-century house on a semi-rural site in Wilmslow, Cheshire. The roughcast brick walls include a projecting portion rising to four gables and with applied half-timbering. The roof is covered with Lake District Slate.

b. This house, bearing a datestone of 1925, is situated opposite 133a. The brick walls are pebble-dashed; there is a prominent gabled tall entry porch and there are two dormers partly in the roof space. There is no hint of imitation half-timbering, or indeed of recognisably local vernacular details in a house of high architectural quality.

c. Cottages in Pershore, Worcestershire. These houses of the 1950s or 1960s echo the brick prevailing in the town, but otherwise the design is based on its period rather than its location.

d. House on an estate in Wilmslow, Cheshire, 1982. Here is a brick and tiled detached house with applied half-timbering which echoes the square-panelled timber-frame construction traditional in the county.

town ideal, the New Towns were initially intended to have populations of 50,000 but these targets were increased. Later generations of New Towns were based on existing towns such as Warrington and culminated in the huge Milton Keynes in Buckinghamshire.

Interwar Housing

The houses designed by the Vernacular Revival architects were mostly for the middle classes and on spacious rural or suburban sites, but their architects did take an interest in the design of small houses and cottages at the request of clients, such as at Port Sunlight, or in response to competitions as at Letchworth. The great spread of suburbs occurred during the period between the two World Wars and house designs were derived from the work of these architects. The Vernacular Revival characteristics of wide, low elevations with hipped roofs and cross gables, pebble-dashed walls, prominent chimney stacks, bay windows, leaded lights or small panes of glass, portions of imitation half-timbering, all filtered down through the work of local architects or builders' draughtsmen providing type plans. The designs of Voysey seemed to be especially easy to adapt. Site layouts depended on curving roads and cul-de-sac patterns; houses enjoyed wide frontage; room heights were much less than in Victorian terrace houses; first-floor rooms were partly in the roof space giving low eaves and a 'cottagey' impression. The semi-detached house proved very popular, having the practical advantage of allowing easy access to the back garden with its dustbins and vegetable plot and the further benefit of room for a garage for the increasing numbers who enjoyed such a luxury. Visually the semi-detached pair allowed for the sought-after low horizontal designs. Half-timbering was not structural, the timbers were applied to brick walls but still took note of a long-abandoned, but once important, technique. The affection for pebble-dash is less easy to explain and may relate to the Scottish work of Lorimer.

Most of the interwar suburban houses were privately built, usually by developers of housing estates and including the great national building firms. They were generally built without subsidy but benefitted from a well-organised mortgage market by way of the building societies. However, there were also 'council houses', subsidized dwellings often built in conjunction with slum clearance projects, helping the poorer city residents to gain the benefits of a semi-rural life. Some of these estates, such as those of the London County Council, were on a large scale and Wythenshawe was developed as a municipal New Town by the City of Manchester. All included terraced as well as semi-detached houses and entailed a greater degree of uniformity in house design with a leaning towards the Neo-Georgian, as in Liverpool.

Whether Vernacular Revival or Neo-Georgian in inclination the suburban houses of the interwar period paid only limited acknowledgment at best to the vernacular architecture of the neighbourhood. Even building materials tended to uniformity throughout the country with designs based fundamentally on the timber-frame and brick of the South East of England.

Housing after the Second World War

The optimism which characterised government and people during the Second World War led to reports and proposals for the better organising of post-war housing. A comprehensive planning system and a big New Towns programme were expected to help correct defects such as ribbon development. Social studies and studies of domestic life led to the Housing Manuals of 1944 and 1949; they concentrated on house planning rather than on their appearance, though a study of the architectural use of building materials stressed the benefits and economy of using local materials. For new buildings in the countryside, whether village infill and expansion or agricultural workers' cottages, regional characteristics and local materials were recommended. The architects Tayler and Green, working mainly for district councils in Norfolk, designed modern houses, mainly in terraces, which now after forty years or more seem both modern and yet in character.

The 1950s and 1960s witnessed a decline in affection for the Vernacular Revival as Modern Architecture influenced designers of local authority or New Town domestic buildings. Designs, vaguely Swedish in concept, with white-painted weatherboard or tile-hanging accompanied by low-pitched roofs and nominal chimneys, were found at this time.

The changing proportions of private as against subsidised housing led to a return to the cozy feeling and general charm of houses inspired by the Vernacular Revival. Brick walls and tiled roofs became general; bay windows and deep eaves enlivened the elevations; imitation half-timbering returned. However, attempts to control the 'free for all' in housing design were led by Essex County Council with their Design Guide, which gave recommendations on proportions and choice of materials so as to relate the design of new houses to the Essex vernacular. This undoubtedly had an effect in the county and other local authorities followed suit with varying success. Another attempt to influence housing design and layout was by model developments such as Poundsbury near Dorchester, sponsored by the Prince of Wales, which closely followed local vernacular designs. Another movement was one that paid close attention to the best practices in conservation and infill in existing villages and small towns, whereby the new houses and refurbished old houses shared traditional designs, materials and constructional details. This may be seen most convincingly in some of the stone-bearing regions such as the Cotswolds, the Pennines and the Lake District. Within the towns and on their outskirts the same movement has led to a revival of polychromatic brick decoration and a return to the use of terraced housing.

Conclusion

We have seen that as vernacular architecture, according to generally accepted definitions, died out in this country in the latter half of the nineteenth century so a number of revivals in architecture took place culminating in the Vernacular Revival Movement associated with C. F. A. Voysey and a number of his contemporaries. They worked for individual clients on houses of more than average size on mainly rural sites. With the spread of the suburbs, especially throughout the twentieth century, the designs of the Vernacular Revival Movement were adapted by the builders working through their architects and draughtsmen to give the domestic feeling which the householders expected. Other styles were adopted, especially by local authority architects and those working on New Towns, but by the close of the twentieth century the influence of the Vernacular Revival movement of a century or more ago is still all-pervasive. Few designs were direct copies of vernacular buildings; few designs adopted vernacular details in a particularly scholarly manner; garages lacked any vernacular precedent. The vernacular which gave inspiration was generally a confection of designs and details from the South of England but, nevertheless, at several removes the vernacular buildings of the countryside had provided that inspiration.

The present-day vernacular is not a rebirth of the true vernacular of past centuries, it is based on a revival in polite architecture of the true vernacular, but if we can adapt definitions to new circumstances then the Vernacular Revival, considerably modified, is the popular or vernacular architecture of our time.

Further Developments

134. House in Dacre, Cumbria
This house, built in 2000, is of traditional proportions, materials and architectural details.

135. House in the style of a barn conversion, Hertingfordbury, Hertfordshire
This well-proportioned house has been designed to fit into its farm setting.

Bibliography

Comprehensive bibliographies on the subject of vernacular architecture have been published from time to time since 1972 by the Vernacular Architecture Group. The following is a selection of books whereby various aspects of the study may be pursued in greater depth. Each book contains its own bibliography or list of references for even deeper study.

Some general works

S. O. Addy, *The Evolution of the English House*, revd. edn. of 1933, re-issued 1975

N. W. Alcock, *Cruck Construction: An Introduction and Catalogue*, 1981

N. W. Alcock, *Documenting the History of Houses*, 2003

N. W. Alcock and Linda Hall, *Fixtures and Fittings in Dated Houses, 1567–1763*, 1994

J. Ayres, *Domestic Interiors: The British Tradition, 1500–1850*, 2003

M. W. Barley, *The English Farmhouse and Cottage*, 1961

M. W. Barley, *Houses and History*, 1986

P. S. Barnwell and C. Giles (for RCHME), *English Farmsteads 1750–1914*, 1997

E. Beaton, *Scotland's Traditional Houses*, 1997

R. W. Brunskill, *Timber Building in Britain*, 2nd edn., 1994

R. W. Brunskill, *Houses and Cottages of Britain*, 1997

R. W. Brunskill, *Brick Building in Britain*, 2nd edn., 1997

R. W. Brunskill, *Traditional Farm Buildings of Britain and their Conservation*, 1999

R. W. Brunskill, *Vernacular Architecture: an Illustrated Handbook*, 2000

S. D. Chapman (ed.), *The History of Working-Class Housing*, 1971

F. W. B. Charles, *Medieval Cruck-building and its Derivatives*, 1967

A. Clifton-Taylor, *The Pattern of English Building*, 4th definitive edn., 1987

A. L. Cummings, *The Framed Houses of Massachusetts Bay*, 1979

J. Grenville, *Medieval Housing*, 1997

R. Harris, *Discovering Timber-framed Buildings*, 1979

N. Harvey, *A History of Farm Buildings in England and Wales*, 2nd, edn., 1984

C. A. Hewett, *English Historic Carpentry*, 1980

C. F. Innocent, *The Development of English Building Construction*, 1916, re-issued 1999

D. Iredale and J. Barrett, *Discovering Your Old House*, 4th edn., 2002

J. Lowe, *Welsh Industrial Workers' Housing, 1775–1875*, 1977

J. Lowe, *Welsh Country Workers' Housing, 1775–1875*, 1985

J. McCann, *Clay and Cob Buildings*, 3rd edn., 2004

E. Mercer, *English Vernacular Houses*, 1975

S. Muthesius, *The English Terraced House*, 1982

R. J. Naismith, *Buildings of the Scottish Countryside*, 1985

S. Pearson and B. Meeson (eds.), *Vernacular Buildings in a Changing World*, 2001

I. C. Peate, *The Welsh House*, 3rd edn., 1946

J. and J. Penoyre, *Houses in the Landscape*, 1978

J. E. C. Peters, *Discovering Traditional Farm Buildings*, 1981 and 2003

C. Platt, *The English Medieval Town*, 1976

A. Quiney, *The Traditional Buildings of England*, 1990

A. Quiney, *Town Houses of Medieval Britain*, 2003

J. Reynolds, *Windmills and Watermills*, 1970

B. K. Roberts, *The Making of the English Village*, 1987

L. Smith, *Investigating Old Buildings*, 1985

P. Smith, *Houses of the Welsh Countryside*, 2nd edn., 1989

C. F. Stell (for RCHME), *Nonconformist Chapels and Meeting Houses*, Vols. 1–4 1986–2002

C. Taylor, *Village and Farmstead*, 1983

E. Wiliam, *The Historical Farm Buildings of Wales*, 1986

A. Wright, *Craft Techniques for Traditional Buildings*, 1981

Some Regional Books

P. S. Barnwell and A. T. Adams (for RCHME), *The House Within: Interpreting Medieval Houses in Kent*, 1994

P. Beacham (ed.), *Devon Building*, 1990

R. W. Brunskill, *Traditional Buildings of Cumbria*, 2002

L. Caffyn (for RCHME), *Workers' Housing in West Yorkshire*, 1986

R. Cousins, *Lincolnshire Buildings in the Mud and Stud Tradition*, 2000

S. Denyer, *Traditional Buildings and Life in the Lake District*, 1991

Sir Cyril Fox and Lord Raglan, *Monmouthshire Houses*, 1951, 1953, 1954

C. Giles (for RCHME), *Rural Houses of West Yorkshire*, 1986

L. Hall, *The Rural Houses of North Avon and South Gloucestershire*, 1983

J. Harding, *Four Centuries of Charlwood Houses*, 1976

B. Harrison and B. Hutton, *Vernacular Houses in North Yorkshire and Cleveland*, 1984

D. and B. Martin, *Historic Buildings in Eastern Sussex*, Vols. 1–5 1978–1985

G. Miller, *Historic Houses in Lancashire: The Douglas Valley, 1300–1770*, 2002

M. Moran, *Vernacular Buildings of Shropshire*, 2003

S. Pearson (for RCHME), *Rural Houses of the Lancashire Pennines*, 1985

S. Pearson (for RCHME), *The Medieval Houses of Kent*, 1994

E. Roberts, *Hampshire Houses, 1250–1700, their dating and development*, 2003

Royal Commission on the Historical Monuments of England, *Houses of the North York Moors*, 1987

P. M. Slocombe, *Wiltshire Farmhouses and Cottages, 1500–1800*, 1998

P. M. Slocombe, *Wiltshire Farm Buildings, 1500–1850*, 1989

P. M. Slocombe, *Medieval Houses of Wiltshire*, 1992

J. T. Smith (for RCHME), *English Houses, 1200–1800: The Hertfordshire Evidence*, 1992

J. Warren (ed.), *Wealden Buildings*, 1990

R. B. Wood-Jones, *Traditional Domestic Architecture of the Banbury Region*, 1963

Some references for Chapter 11

A. M. Edwards, *The Design of Suburbia*, 1981
H. Muthesius, *The English House*, 1904, 1908; English edn., 1979
J. M. Richards, *The Castles on the Ground*, 1946; 2nd edn., 1973
W. S. Sparrow (ed.), *The British Home of Today*, 1904
W. S. Sparrow (ed.), *The Modern Home*, 1906
G. Stamp, *The English House, 1860–1914*, 1980

In addition to the thematic volumes noted above, the county by county *Inventories* of the Royal Commissions on Historic Monuments of England, Scotland and Wales contain much material on the subject. By far the most comprehensive in this connection is the publication of the Royal Commission on the Ancient and Historical Monuments of Wales, *Inventory of Ancient Monuments in Glamorgan*, Vol. IV, part 2: Farmhouses and Cottages, 1988.

A great deal of material on vernacular architecture consists of articles in journals of various sorts. The main periodical in this country exclusively devoted to the subject is *Vernacular Architecture*, the annual journal of the Vernacular Architecture Group. Among the national journals which regularly publish articles on the subject are the following:

The Archaeological Journal, published by the Royal Archaeological Institute
The Journal of the British Archaeological Association
Folk Life, published by the Society for Folk Life Studies
The Journal of the Historic Farm Buildings Group
Medieval Archaeology, published by the Society for Medieval Archaeology
Post-Medieval Archaeology, published by the Society for Post-Medieval Archaeology
Transactions of the Ancient Monuments Society
Vernacular Building, published by the Scottish Vernacular Buildings Working Group

Nearly all the county archaeological and antiquarian societies publish articles on vernacular architecture from time to time in their transactions. For instance, the series of articles on 'The Houses of Breconshire', by J. T. Smith and S. R. Jones, published in *Brycheiniog*, the Journal of the Brecknock Society between 1963 and 1969, add up to a substantial volume on the domestic vernacular architecture of that county.

Index